It happened in
GLOUCESTERSHIRE

PRORSUM SEMPER

Phyllida Barstow

Merlin Unwin Books

First published in Great Britain by Merlin Unwin Books, 2011
Text © Phyllida Barstow, 2011

Published by:
Merlin Unwin Books Ltd
Palmers House
7 Corve Street
Ludlow
Shropshire SY8 1DB
U.K.

www.merlinunwin.co.uk

The author asserts her moral right to be identified with this work.
Designed and set in Bembo by Merlin Unwin
Printed in Great Britain by TJ International Ltd, Padstow, Cornwall

ISBN 978 1 906122 30 0

PHYLLIDA BARSTOW, who has lived on a very small farm
near Uley in Gloucestershire for the past 25 years, is the author of
six historical novels, five adventure novels, two social histories and
a couple of biographies. Her recent account of her rural childhood
from 1937–56, *My Animals and Other Family*, was described by Joanna
Trollope as 'a refreshingly candid account'. Phyllida has also written
numerous columns for sporting magazines.

CONTENTS

THE COUNTY OF GLOUCESTERSHIRE

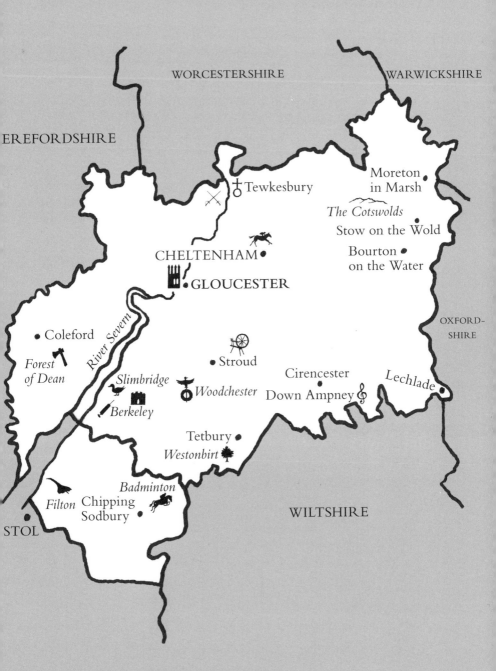

WORCESTERSHIRE

WARWICKSHIRE

EREFORDSHIRE

Tewkesbury

Moreton
in Marsh

The Cotswolds

Stow on the Wold

CHELTENHAM

Bourton
on the Water

GLOUCESTER

OXFORD-
SHIRE

Coleford

River Severn

*Forest
of Dean*

Stroud

Cirencester

Lechlade

Slimbridge

Woodchester

Down Ampney

Berkeley

Tetbury

Westonbirt

Badminton

Filton Chipping
Sodbury

WILTSHIRE

STOL

To all our friends in
Gloucestershire

Chapter One

EARLY GLOUCESTERSHIRE
Who lived here first – and why?

From the lush pastures of the Severn Vale to the high, bare, stone-walled Cotswold plateau, along the steep and indented escarpment and then down through its winding broken valleys to the wooded secrecy of the Forest of Dean, Gloucestershire has a rich and diverse landscape whose promise of trading and agricultural opportunities was recognised by the earliest tribes to inhabit the area, and all who followed them.

This rough rectangle of a county has an area of nearly a million and a half acres and, being strategically positioned between Oxfordshire in the east, Wiltshire in the south, and Worcestershire in the north, with Herefordshire and the Welsh Marches to the west, it has particularly good motorway links to both north and west by virtue of the M5, and to London via the M4.

Far from being a natural landscape, Gloucestershire's beautiful countryside has been shaped by the activities of the people who have made their living from the land over the past four thousand years, so that every grassed-over track, every wood, every field has its own story to tell – if only we could hear it.

Outside the busy, thriving towns and beyond the roar of

modern traffic lies a gentler, more peaceful world, where the lovely tracery of dry-stone walls crisscrossing the old sheep-walks bears witness to uncountable hours of skilled work, constantly renewed as sections collapsed and had to be restored, while isolated farms and villages huddled against valley slopes blend so perfectly in their surroundings that they seem to have grown from the soil itself.

Over the ages successive waves of invaders ranging from Celtic tribesmen to twenty-first century film stars and Russian oligarchs have settled in the Cotswolds and taken possession of the land they needed to mould into their own patches of heaven.

Everard Parry and his son Ryan still practise the ancient craft of dry stone walling in the country around Minchinhampton. Gloucestershire's characteristic walls require continual maintenance, and are liable to sudden collapse after frost damage.

As a result you rarely travel more than a few miles without finding a prehistoric barrow, iron age fort, Roman villa, Saxon church or Norman castle to bring the past vividly to mind. Nearer our own time, magnificent cathedrals and noblemen's houses recreate the splendours of former ages, and glorious gardens are still being established today.

So much has happened in the county, it contains so many architectural treasures and places of historical interest, and has given birth to such a variety of world-famous figures that any selection must be a purely personal one, chosen to give an overall snapshot of how each area developed its character and appearance.

So who were the peoples who first settled in Gloucestershire, and what made them come here?

Certainly one of the keys to its allure in ancient times was the River Severn – Milton's Sabrina Fair – at over 200 miles the longest river in Britain, which rises in Wales and finally debouches into the Bristol Channel, forming a natural barrier against the wild mountains to the west and the fierce hungry tribes who lived there. Before the establishment of roads and tracks, the Severn was a vital conduit for the transport of goods and people between early trading posts both up and downstream.

There was already an effective system of river traffic in Neolithic times. Around 2,550 BC Stonehenge's famous Bluestones were rafted from the Welsh mountains along the Bristol Channel, then up the rivers Avon and Wylye before being dragged on rollers overland to their destination near Salisbury. It is hard to imagine exactly how our distant ancestors moved these heavy, unwieldy objects such a distance, or guess why they felt it necessary to do so, but no doubt they would look with similar puzzlement on our own costly efforts to reach the moon and stars.

Over the centuries, tribes armed with bronze tools and weapons, came over the sea from the western fringes of the

Continent and gradually displaced Neolithic Man, driving him ever farther into the forests and mountains, until all that was left to remind us of him were the remnants of his henges and standing stones, and the many long barrows, or 'tumps' in which he buried his dead. These 'hollow hills' or 'fairy hills' are spooky places which easily spawn superstitions and legends. Belas Knap near Winchcombe on the edge of the Cotswold escarpment is 178 feet long and 18 feet high and within its four small chambers the remains of 38 bodies are scattered. Hetty Pegler's Tump, above the village of Uley, has a low entrance into which the stout-hearted may crawl, but you are warned not to stay within for more than two minutes, or you may find a whole day and night has passed without your knowledge. Nor must you eat anything there, or the fairies will never let you go...

These early Britons built settlements on high points, for easy defence, and constructed the Iron Age forts that overlook the Berkeley Vale. Their principal tribe, the Dobunni, had its capital at Cirencester, (which later on the Romans also adopted as an important hub of commerce).

Fast forward, then, to Roman times, when a Gloucestershire posting was every centurion's dream compared to the chilly hell of a remote fortress on Hadrian's Wall. Making use of the local workforce to do the heavy lifting, the Romans looked around for the most convenient places to plant their settlements. Most of the far-flung Empire's luxury goods reached Britain via the ports at either end of Watling Street, Dover in the east and Caerleon in the west – the latter being no more than a few days' easy stages by bullock cart from the big Roman camp at Gloucester, whence they were distributed to Cirencester, Towcester, and all the other 'cesters' and 'chesters' (echoing the Latin *castra,* a camp) that maintained the Pax Romana in Britain. Being at the junction of Ermin Street and the Fosse Way, Cirencester was a particularly important hub for commerce.

View from the top of Uley Bury, the Bronze Age fort, looking south-west towards Downham Hill.

Scratch Gloucestershire, find Rome, as the old saying goes, and it is certain that many yet-undiscovered antiquities must still lie beneath the county's fields. The Romans were great builders who liked their comforts, and they built to last. Around Cirencester was the equivalent of the stockbroker belt, where luxurious villas equipped with bath-houses, elaborate shrines, underfloor heating and beautiful mosaic pavements are still being discovered. Though some have been carefully excavated and their treasures recorded, others have simply had their position noted and then been covered over again to preserve them for posterity.

Most spectacular of all is the famous Orpheus pavement which was revealed in all its splendour in the churchyard at Woodchester, near Stroud, in 1793. At 47 foot (14.5 metres) square, it is the largest mosaic yet uncovered, composed of 1.5 million tesserae which depict the lyre-playing Orpheus charming wild birds, fishes and beasts, including lion, tiger, leopard and elephant, with his music.

Constructed around AD 325, towards the end of the Roman occupation, it was designed to decorate the floor of the great hall in a 60-room villa. This must have been the palace of an important official, quite possibly the Governor-General of Western Britain, since Woodchester is almost equidistant between the important towns of Cirencester (Corinium) and Gloucester (Glaevum) with Bath, the R&R spa the Romans called Aqua Sulis, only a day's ride to the south.

The pavement is a work of astonishing beauty and complexity. The design was probably commissioned from the craftsmen at the Corinium School of Mosaicists, and the five basic colours of the tesserae – squares ranging from a quarter of an inch to an inch and a quarter in size – are all available locally. White, yellow, and blue

The working party that uncovered the great mosaic at Woodchester in 1926. The Rector, the Reverend Arthur Pink, is in the back row.

limestone comes from nearby quarries, the ginger sandstone from the Forest of Dean, and red from fired clay tiles.

The central octagon almost certainly had a fountain in the middle, and the eighth side of its surrounding guilloche, or plait, is occupied by the figure of Orpheus, whose music charmed all living creatures. He wears a pointed Phrygian cap, and rests his lyre upon one knee, while his billowing cloak gives an impression of wind movement. His dog is close at his side, and round him flutter birds, peacock and pheasant among them, interspersed with leaves and berries. Two more decorative plaits separate him from the wild beasts – lion, tiger, leopard, elephant and a winged heraldic creature – and below them the head of Neptune, adorned with lobster claws, and surrounded by undulating waves of acanthus.

Now the problem arose of turning a round design into a square one, which the mosaicists solved by creating four corners and filling the spandrels with lissom, semi-draped water-nymphs, before resorting to a series of richly detailed geometric designs to complete the elaborate pavement.

Less than a hundred years after the Orpheus mosaic was laid in all its glory, the Romans withdrew from Britain, and it is the greatest pity that the Saxons who succeeded them built a settlement on the site of the Governor's palace. Their church was where the bath-house had been, and the surrounding area of graveyard occupied the same ground as the Orpheus pavement. As the centuries passed and more graves were dug, sections of the mosaic became irreparably damaged.

It was not that it was entirely forgotten. Local people knew it was there, but evidently they could find no practical use for the little colourful tesserae, unlike the remaining clay bricks and tiles of the villa, which were recycled into the walls of the church.

From time to time it was referred to by travellers or diarists, for instance by Bishop Gibson who, writing in 1695, called it a famous monument, 'having birds, beasts, and flowers all in small stones a little bigger than dice'; and in the early 18th century it was partially uncovered by successive antiquarians, who left drawings of what they had seen.

However, it was not until 1793 that the artist and antiquarian Samuel Lyson, the foremost archaeologist of the day, spent four years excavating the site, drawing, measuring, and recording what he found. His *Account of the Roman Antiquities Discovered at Woodchester* is a model of precision and accuracy, and eager crowds flocked to see the marvellous pavement for themselves.

Its popularity, indeed, became a problem. Woodchester lies in a steep and narrow valley, and crowds of sightseers quickly jam up the little winding approach roads. Since 1793, the pavement has been uncovered for short periods at least a dozen times, with the problem of access and exit becoming worse every time, and when in 1973 some 140,000 visitors came to view it over a two-month period, local traffic was so badly disrupted that a decision was taken to cover it up for good beneath hundreds of tons of sand, soil, and turf.

Meantime, however, the brothers Bob and John Woodward had spent ten years in the mammoth, self-imposed task of constructing a complete replica, using 1.6 million hand–cut clay blocks on sheets of hardboard which could be moved and displayed in different venues. In June 2010, the entire replica pavement was sold at auction, though a suitable site on which to exhibit it has yet to be found.

The Roman legions left Britain in AD 410, to attend to troubles nearer home, but although the Roman way of life continued in Gloucestershire for at least another century and a half, the Germanic tribe of Saxons and the Angles, from Denmark, who gradually took over their territory, went about establishing their rule in a very different way. Like encroaching brambles moving from east to west, they leapfrogged forward in small advances

Part of the animal circle of the great Orpheus mosaic in the Roman Villa at Woodchester. In Greek mythology Orpheus, who is featured in the centre of the composition, charmed all nature with his music.

and, unlike the Romans, where they put down roots they stayed. Therefore it was not until the battle of Dyrham in 577 that they captured the city of Gloucester, which had fallen on hard times since its glory days as a *colonia* of the Roman Empire.

During the fifth and sixth centuries these polytheistic pagans were, by degrees, converted to Christianity, with the strongest resistance to the new religion coming from the serfs and the greatest enthusiasm from the nobility. Between these social extremes, the Saxon freemen, who were tidy farmers and good stockmen, established the great sheep-walks which supplied the woollen trade that became Gloucestershire's principal export for centuries, while their nimble-fingered women perfected the crafts of spinning and weaving.

The wide expanses of high, gently undulating 'wold' with

fine short grass and turf that never grew soggy could supply the needs of countless thousands of sheep. Abbeys and monasteries raised huge flocks of the leggy, fine-fleeced sheep they called 'Cotswold Lions', whose wool hung in corkscrew ringlets and could be woven into excellent cloth, and with the proceeds they built handsome churches all over Gloucestershire.

Saxons set less store on their comforts than Romans, and the wooden palaces built by their noblemen lasted less well. Whether freemen or serfs, the peasants lived in rudimentary cabins, often built over a shallow pit filled with straw for warmth, with wattle-plastered walls and a thatched roof with a hole through which smoke from the fire could escape, not unlike today's African shambas. These frequently caught fire accidentally – or were

Minchinhampton Common, a 580-acre swathe of high open grassland with public grazing rights. It is the site of prehistoric fields, numerous burial mounds and the remains of an ancient earthwork known as The Bulwarks.

deliberately burned by Viking raiders, whose much-dreaded longships would glide up the Bristol Channel and wreak havoc inland.

This was one good reason for the Saxons to add towers to their substantial stone churches, less for the glory of God than as a good lookout point. Sometimes the tower was equipped with a ladder which could be drawn up to prevent the raiders climbing it. Few Saxon churches remain in Gloucestershire, though a sharp eye can detect parts of them which have been incorporated into later buildings. Triangular rough-hewn stones around window-embrasures are one giveaway, as are pillars constructed in alternating horizontal and vertical layers.

However one village, Deerhurst, still boasts not one but two recognisably Saxon buildings, St Mary's Church and Odda's chapel, which is now incorporated in a farmhouse, but was once part of a palace.

Finer still are the ruins of St Oswald's Priory in Gloucester itself, where the redoubtable Lady Aethelflaed, daughter of Alfred the Great, re-used stone from a nearby Roman temple to build a shrine for the relics of St Oswald, King of Northumbria, whose bones – minus skull and arms – she and her brother recovered in a daring raid on Viking territory around 900 AD.

Those bones, at least, were able to rest in peace, though other parts of poor St Oswald were widely distributed by monks seeking ownership of their miracle-working powers. The bones of his right arm were stolen from Bamburgh, and taken to Peterborough, where a very narrow chapel was built for them, with a monk blocking the entrance twenty-four hours a day in case anyone tried to take them back north. His head – or what was said to be his head – was buried in Durham Cathedral, though at least four other heads at different European locations are claimed as St Oswald's.

So the Saxon agriculturalists – both the early pagans and later churchgoing Christians – ploughed their way through Gloucester-shire history during the post-Roman Dark Ages, squabbling with their neighbours over boundaries from time to time, but leaving it to a succession of kings with unpronounceable names to take ever more of England under their control. Alfred the Great's laws served them well until the fateful year of 1066, when England's king, the childless Edward the Confessor, who had previously offered the throne to William, Duke of Normandy, changed his mind on his deathbed and named Harold, Earl Godwin as his successor instead.

Furious at being superseded, the Duke of Normandy launched an invasion, landing near Hastings in October 1066 and, in the battle which followed, killed King Harold and changed for ever the course of English history.

Chapter Two

AFTER THE CONQUEST

In Gloucestershire, as in the rest of England, William the Conqueror's invasion was not unexpected. For months King Harold's fyrds, or troops, had been on guard duty on the South Coast, but unfortunately when the Normans eventually set sail in September many of the fyrds had been allowed to return home to help with the harvest, while Harold himself had hurriedly taken his remaining fighting force of huscarls and thegns to the north-east, where another claimant to the throne, Harald Hardrada, had joined forces with Tostig Godwinson, Harold's younger brother, to launch an invasion.

Marching day and night, Harold's army covered 185 miles in four days, to take the Norwegian invaders by surprise at Stamford Bridge, in east Yorkshire. In the battle that ensued on September 25th, 1066, both Hardrada and Tostig were killed, and only 24 ships of the 300-strong invading fleet carried home survivors.

It was a decisive victory, but Harold had no chance to celebrate. Exhausted and battered as his men were, he hurried them south again to face the challenge from Duke William of Normandy, but this second ferocious battle within three weeks had a very different outcome. On 14th October 1066, King Harold was killed at the Battle of Hastings, and ten weeks later, on Christmas Day, William the Conqueror had himself crowned king in Westminster Abbey.

After the coronation, things moved fast. William doled out great tracts of land to his barons, who hurried off north, south, east and west to secure their new domains. Gloucestershire and a large area surrounding it was assigned to his loyal follower Robert Fitzhamon, who was unusual in remaining faithful not only to William I, but also to his fiery-headed, fiery-tempered third son, William Rufus, who succeeded him in 1087.

Fitzhamon it was who warned William Rufus of a plot to kill him while out hunting and, when his warning was ignored, it is said that Fitzhamon was the first to weep over the body of that unlovable monarch when he was found dead in his New Forest, felled by an arrow shot accidentally-on-purpose by Sir Walter Tyrell.

William the Conqueror himself had been born a bastard, though named as his father's heir at the age of seven, and many of his followers were adventurous younger sons who would not otherwise have inherited large estates. They did not take possession unopposed – far from it. Rebellions were frequent in the first years of transition from Anglo-Saxon to Norman rule and eventually the Pope was moved to reprimand William for his brutal mistreatment of the English.

Slowly the country resigned itself to the inevitable and recognised that the Normans had come to stay. The new rulers intermarried with the old Anglo-Saxon nobility, and though the incoming overlords were ruthless in enforcing laws regarding their own hunting rights, from the point of view of a serf there was not much difference between being owned by a Norman baron or an Anglo-Saxon thegn.

Though the new rulers spoke French among themselves, the English – as Anglo-Saxons now regarded themselves – have always had a special knack for corrupting foreign languages and our ancestors soon evolved their own version of the tongue. Very quickly Beau Desert became Bewdesie and Bel Voir Beever, while Fleur de lys morphed gently into Flower Dellis. Legal documents were drawn up in Latin, the European lingua franca which all educated men understood.

The Conqueror's grants of land had bought his barons' loyalty to the crown, but they were a quarrelsome, acquisitive bunch. No matter how much they were given, they always wanted more, and when their wishes were thwarted, they were quick to rebel.

William de Braose, to whom the Conqueror granted the land west of Hungerford to the Welsh Marches is still remembered for the chain of castles he built to keep the rebellious Welsh subjugated.

The remains of the effigy of the Norman knight William de Braose in the nave of St Mary's Church, Tetbury.

He, too, remained loyal to the king who had rewarded him so well, but a generation later his grandson, another William, the remains of whose effigy still lie in the Church of St Mary at Tetbury, took a different view of his feudal obligations. 'The Ogre of Abergavenny,' as this second William de Braose was known, was brutal and untrustworthy even by the low standards of the day. He earned his nickname by slaughtering Seisyll ap Dynval and a hundred unarmed Welshmen on Christmas Day in Abergavenny Castle.

Subsequently, the Ogre stubbornly refused to pay his dues to King Henry I, who succeeded his brother William Rufus. As a punishment he was outlawed and exiled, his lands forfeited, and his unfortunate wife Maud de Sainte-Valerie, who had borne him sixteen children, was immured in Windsor Castle and deliberately starved to death. You crossed a Norman king at your peril.

The Normans built on a massive scale. Large numbers of their square-towered churches and sturdy fortresses have stood the test of time so well that Gloucestershire is a medieval historian's delight, still plentifully supplied with relics of the Conqueror's dynasty, though in the case of the castles different conflicts down the ages have left their mark in the form of battered walls and breached defences.

One of the few to escape unscathed is Berkeley Castle, which deserves a chapter of its own.

Chapter Three

SPLENDOUR IN STONE

Berkeley Castle

Imagine a perfect medieval fortress, complete with towers and battlements, motte and bailey, a keep some 60 feet tall, narrow winding stairs with special trip-steps to make invaders stumble, a magnificent Great Hall, and a fearsome dungeon, and there you have Berkeley Castle, the oldest continuously occupied non-royal castle in England, built 850 years ago and still going strong.

It is one of the chain of Marcher castles that stretched the length of the Welsh border, splendidly sited on an eminence just to the south-east of the town of Berkeley, overlooking the Severn to keep watch on the Welsh across the river. The tower commands a wide swathe of the river banks and surrounding country, which could be flooded if necessary for defensive purposes. Most astonishing of all is the fact that it has been owned and occupied by the same family since Norman times.

When William the Conqueror embarked on the task of settling his new kingdom and establishing its exact extent, the Domesday Book which he commissioned records the grant of estates at Berkeley to the family of FitzOsbern, Earl of Hereford, who adopted the name of his new possession. The first Roger de Berkeley was only a reeve, or royal tax collector, but very soon he became lessee of the Berkeley estates, though never a baron.

Although three generations later the Berkeley family fell out with King Henry II, and he granted the Castle as a reward to Robert Fitzharding, who had bankrolled his successful invasion of England during the final phase of the long-drawn-out conflict between Stephen and Matilda, the link with the original family remained, since Fitzharding's son married one of Roger de Berkeley's daughters.

Most of the building of this massive fortification, which has seen much historical drama, took place in the 1150s and '60s. The keep and towers surround a large courtyard about 140 yards in circumference, entered beneath a machicolated gatehouse. One side of the court is the great baronial hall, which has magnificent exposed beams and is hung with ancient tapestries, and another tower of the keep contains the dungeon chamber where King Edward II was confined in 1327 and eventually murdered.

It was the misfortune of this wayward, artistic monarch, who came to the throne in 1307, that not only was his powerful, successful father Edward I – who had subdued the Welsh and was known as the Hammer of the Scots – a hard act to follow, but that his own homosexual leanings made him an object of contempt to the turbulent English barons, who were always ready to exploit any weakness in their liege lord.

Nor did Edward ll attempt to hide his proclivities: on the contrary he gave most of the jewels which his 12 year old bride, Isabel of France, had received as wedding gifts, to his own favourite, handsome Piers Gaveston, whom he had recalled from exile in France as soon as his father died.

Young as she was, Isabella – as she is known to us – was outraged by this treatment and mortified to find that her new husband ignored her in favour of Gaveston, but she accepted the situation and became friends with Gaveston. She remained a loyal wife and bore her husband four children before 1325, when she eventually joined the coalition of barons determined to depose

Edward. He had been disastrously defeated by the Scots at the battle of Bannockburn in 1314, and his kingdom was sliding into chaos.

Though the barons had murdered Gaveston, his place as Edward's favourite had soon been filled by Hugh Despencer who, like his father (another Hugh) was a Marcher lord detested by the barons' coalition.

Isabella persuaded her husband to send her to France as an ambassador to her brother, now the French king, to prevent him from seizing England's French possessions. Crucially, Edward allowed her to take with her their eldest son, his heir, to do homage on his behalf. With the young prince safely beyond his father's reach, Isabella – later known as the She-Wolf of France – was free to plot his downfall with her lover Roger Mortimer, the Earl of March, and raise an army to invade England.

Reluctant to start an unnecessary and expensive war with his brother-in-law and disapproving of his sister's lover, the French king ordered her out of the country, but she didn't go far. Slipping over the border into Hainault, she offered the hand of her fourteen-year-old son to the Count of Hainault's daughter Philippa in exchange for troops with which to depose her husband King Edward.

In 1426, when London failed to rally to his support, the king fled west. He was captured, his favourites the Despencers were gruesomely executed, and the king himself forced to abdicate in favour of his son.

So far so good for Isabella and Mortimer, but a deposed king is an awkward customer to deal with. So long as he lives, rebels and malcontents are likely to use him as a focus and figurehead for their own plots. On the other hand, regicide is not only a particularly heinous crime but also apt to create martyrs, who may prove equally troublesome from beyond the grave.

Uncertain what to do with her husband, Queen Isabella

ordered him to be imprisoned at Kenilworth and, when that caused rumblings of discontent among Edward's still-active supporters in the Welsh Marches, had him conveyed to the high security of Berkeley Castle, with Thomas de Berkeley and Sir John Maltravers as his custodians, while she and her lover considered their next move.

There the unhappy king spent five months lodged in the room still known as his cell. Though treated as a noble guest and allowed his own cook and other servants, he was a captive, and spent his time writing sorrowful religious poems repenting of his sins.

Finally Isabella must have decided that stronger measures were called for. Towards the end of September 1327, while Lord Berkeley was discreetly absent from his castle, Edward II was murdered, probably by suffocation. Stories of a red-hot poker thrust into his bowels are a later invention, and the myth that citizens of Berkeley heard his dying screams cannot possibly be true. The castle walls are far too thick for that.

After the King's death was announced, there remained the problem of where to bury him. Westminster Abbey petitioned for the honour, but Mortimer was anxious to avoid potential trouble during a long journey across the country, so Edward was buried in the most prestigious local abbey.

The Abbot of Gloucester sent a procession of monks and well-mounted armed retainers to Berkeley Castle, escorting a richly-draped coffin on a bier. The heart of the murdered king was enclosed in a silver casket, his body embalmed and laid in a lead-lined coffin, and conveyed with due pomp back to Gloucester, with members of the Berkeley family in the procession.

Both the Queen and her son, now Edward III, attended the funeral, and when the new king commissioned the magnificent effigy in Purbeck marble and Nottingham alabaster (the first time this material had been used in the tomb of an English king) under

26

a triple canopy, it became a shrine to which pilgrims flocked, and proved a turning point in the church's fortunes.

Though Lord Berkeley was declared innocent of any wrongdoing in the matter of the king's death, it is perhaps significant that soon afterwards both the Queen and her lover Mortimer were once more being entertained at Berkeley Castle, though they probably kept well away from the dungeon-chamber.

It was during the next century that a long-running inheritance dispute over the Castle and its lands, which had rumbled on unresolved for two generations, finally came to a head with the death in 1468 of the Countess of Shrewsbury. She had long been at loggerheads with William, the 12th Lord Berkeley ('two merciless natures not unevenly encountering,' as one commentator puts it) each encouraging their retainers to fight and raid one another's manors, and when she died her cause was taken up with vigour by her grandson, Thomas Talbot, Lord Lisle.

He was only twenty, recently married to the Earl of Pembroke's daughter, hasty-tempered, impetuous and impatient, determined to settle the dispute once and for all, and the encounter in which the two sides came to blows is often referred to as the last pitched battle between private armies on English soil.

There are at least two versions of events leading to the Battle of Nibley Green. In the simpler and more likely scenario, Lord Lisle with a small number of armed tenants was ambushed and killed by a stronger force led by Lord Berkeley. Lisle's manor was sacked and burned, and his young wife was so distraught that she gave birth to a dead child. End of the Lisle claim to Berkeley land. End of story.

The second version, as outlined in Smyth's *Lives*, is an altogether more elaborate affair. In it, Lord Lisle enlists the help of a traitor within the Berkeley ranks, one Thomas Holt, official Keeper of Berkeley Castle and Whitcliff Park, who bribes the porter with the offer of well-paid employment in Lord Lisle's service if he will open the Castle gates to him.

At the last moment, however, the porter loses his nerve and confesses the scheme to Lord Berkeley, and in his fury at the miscarriage of his plot, Lisle challenges Berkeley to a duel, man to man.

Back at once comes Berkeley's answer. A duel would not settle a legal dispute over inheritance, but why not fight it out in battle? He is prepared to meet all the forces his opponent can muster at Nibley Green, halfway between Berkeley and Wotton, at eight the following morning and, he adds, he himself will not bring one-tenth of the men available to him.

Still seething with fury, Lisle agrees.

What Berkeley fails to mention in his challenge is that he plans to call on his brother's armed retainers from Thornbury as well as his own; nor does he admit that he has already sent a message to Bristol and another to the much-feared miners in the Forest of Dean. The result is that while Lisle barely manages to scrape up three hundred fighters from among his tenants, most of whom have no armour, Berkeley's army numbers a thousand men.

The scene is set for a rout.

Berkeley hides most of his army overnight among the trees of Michaelwood, adjoining Nibley Green, where local people bring them food. When young Lord Lisle is seen riding at the head of his troops down the hill towards the ford at Fowles Grove, (now Foley's Grove), the Berkeley cohorts emerge in strength from the trees and run to meet them.

Before Lisle can even get his visor down, a hail of arrows flies across the stream. Lisle is struck in the side of the face by a Dean forester, who finishes his work with a dagger through the joints in the fallen leader's armour. Lisle's supporters turn and flee back up the narrow lane, with the Berkeley men hot on their heels, hacking and stabbing.

Berkeley Castle, a 12th century fortification designed for keeping the Welsh out of England.

The sack of the Manor, and Lady Lisle's subsequent miscarriage are common to both versions of this brief and bloody affair, but there are implausibilities in the second story. It would, for instance, have been impossible for Berkeley to gather forces from Thornbury, near Bristol, and the Forest of Dean, to the west of the Severn, within a single day. Nor is it likely that Lord Lisle would have approached the ford with his visor up, or surrendered the advantage of higher ground. The evidence for the Holt plot is a single document at the Castle, purporting to be a copy of the plot documents, and the challenge and reply. Experts believe it to be pure invention, concocted later to use as evidence when Lady Lisle sued Lord Berkeley for the murder of her husband.

Whatever the truth, it is certain that less than twenty years later, when Henry VII wrested the crown from Richard III, he took legal steps to ensure there should be no more pitched battles to settle quarrels between his subjects by disbanding and disarming all private armies.

Throughout the next four hundred years Berkeley Castle entertained many exalted visitors, including Queen Elizabeth I, and accumulated many treasures and objects of historical interest that can still be seen by today's visitors. In 1643, when the Civil War was raging in Gloucestershire, the Castle was first garrisoned by the Royalist Army, but after a nine-day siege the wall was breached and it surrendered to Oliver Cromwell's Parliamentarians. Surprisingly, the Berkeley family was allowed to retain possession providing they never repaired the damaged wall – a condition which was enacted by Parliament and is still in force today.

Within the Castle the family lived in considerable state, banqueting in the Great Hall to the music of minstrels, and it was

The courtyard and Great Hall of Berkeley Castle: over 800 years old and still owned by the Berkeley family.

there that a fatal accident befell England's last court jester, Dicky Pearce, who was born in 1665, and had long been the Earl of Suffolk's family fool. The medieval equivalent of today's stand-up comics, jesters were great gossips, always in the know, and though their jokes often had a sharp edge they were allowed a good deal of latitude. After he fell to his death from the minstrels' gallery at Berkeley Castle in 1728, he was buried in the churchyard of St Mary's in Berkeley. His tomb, inscribed with a wry valedictory verse, also bears the epitaph: *My lord that's gone himself made much of him.*

Fast forward, then, to the late 18th century *cause celebre* concerning the Berkeley family which enthralled Georgian England. Over the years since the Battle of Nibley Green, the head of the family's title had become variously Baron, Marquis, Viscount, and Earl as merit and royal favour dictated, and it was during the Fifth Earl's tenure of Berkeley Castle that the seeds of the legal imbroglio were planted.

At Lambeth on May 6th, 1796, Frederick Augustus, 5th Earl of Berkeley, married the beautiful Mary Cole, daughter of an innkeeper from Wotton, near Gloucester. The ceremony was rather belated since the happy couple were already the parents of four sons. After the birth of a fifth son in November 1796, who naturally took precedence over his elder brothers since they had been born out of wedlock, the Earl attempted in 1801 to legitimise his bastard children by claiming that he had married their mother in a private ceremony at Berkeley way back in 1785 – and there for the moment, the matter rested.

After the death of Frederick Augustus, however, in 1810, his eldest pre-marriage son, Colonel William Berkeley, who had inherited the Castle and its lands under his father's will, tried to lay claim to the earldom, and so began what became known as the Berkeley Peerage Case, heard by the Committee of Privileges of the House of Lords.

Appearing for the Claimant were two eminent barristers, Sir Samuel Romilly and Mr Sergeant Best, while the interests of the youngest sons were represented by the Attorney-General and the Solicitor-General, counsels for the Crown.

So devoted was Mary Cole, now the widowed Countess, to her eldest son that she was prepared to swear that she had indeed been married to Frederick Augustus in a private ceremony in the church in Berkeley long before their more public wedding in Lambeth in 1796, and to back up her assertion the Claimant's counsel produced what was alleged to be a leaf torn out of the parish register, with a formal entry of marriage signed by the officiating priest – who had unfortunately just died. The entry was witnessed by one William Tudor – who turned out to be William Cole, Mary's brother – and someone called Barnes – who could not be found.

Further alleged documentation was produced in the form of a register of publication of the banns of marriage which, as the Crown counsel remarked, 'consorted ill with the alleged desire for concealment.' It was, naturally, signed by the same priest.

The Committee of Privileges threw out the case, declaring that the evidence was forged, and when William Berkeley tried another tack, demanding a writ of summons as a baron because he had possession of the Castle, he was told that such baronies were no longer in being, nor likely to be revived.

Despite these setbacks, however, William Berkeley's ceaseless political activity did earn him a peerage twenty years later, when he became Baron Segrave of Berkeley, and, ten years later, Earl Fitzhardinge, but since he died childless, all the legal wrangling over the earldom was ultimately futile. Undeterred, his brother Maurice revived the claim, and was granted a new title of Baron Fitzhardinge of Berkeley, which duly passed to his sons.

One of the most remarkable features of the case, which left Mary Cole's fifth son *de jure* the Sixth Earl of Berkeley, was that in a praiseworthy show of solidarity with his elder brothers, Thomas Moreton Fitzharding Berkeley never assumed or used the title, although he had every right to do so, with the result that the title remained in abeyance until successfully revived by Randal, 8th and last Earl, who died in 1942.

During the tumultuous, war-riven years of the 19th and 20th centuries, the Berkeley family were involved more in local than national politics. This was the era that saw the Castle become a hub of foxhunting and agricultural innovation, with the splendid stabling and kennels for the Berkeley Hunt contained within the walls, and the establishment of Berkeley Hunt Agricultural Society to promote skills among young farmers. The Society's annual Show is still held every August Bank Holiday on the Castle Meadow.

The tomb of court jester Dicky Pearce, in the churchyard of St Mary's, Berkeley.

It was said that in earlier years Lord Berkeley could hunt over his own country from Berkeley Castle to Berkeley Square in London, and certainly he could kennel his hounds on his own property all along this route, (though necessarily he would have had to cross other hunts' countries on the way), and the distinctive mustard livery of the Berkeley Hunt servants has been adopted by other hunts with whom they have been connected, such as the Old Berks and the Vale of Aylesbury.

Jonathan Swift's amusing inscription on the tomb of court jester Dicky Pearce can be seen at St Mary's Church, Berkeley. It reads:

> *Here lies the Earl of Suffolk's fool.*
> *Men call'd him Dicky Pearce.*
> *His Folly serv'd to make folks laugh*
> *When wit and mirth were scarce.*
> *Poor Dick alas is dead and gone.*
> *What signifies to cry?*
> *Dickys enough are still behind*
> *To laugh at by and by.*

As the Castle enters its ninth century, the grandeur of the massive ancient fortifications not only draw great numbers of visitors and tourists, but also act as a magnet for film companies. So if, on your first visit, you have a strange sense of déjà-vu as you gaze at the mighty rosy-purplish walls or turn to look towards the medieval deer-park and across the shining Severn, don't dismiss it as a dream. You may indeed have seen that view before – if only through the camera's eye.

Tewkesbury Abbey

King Henry VIII's 'Vice-Gerent in Spirituals' and fixer-in-chief Thomas Cromwell was a businessman first and foremost and believed in getting value for money. Money for the king, that was. Filling the royal coffers was a never-ending task for the person responsible for the finances of a monarch with a taste for splendour and feminine beauty, not to mention foreign wars.

Searching for a large source of income, Cromwell soon focused on the wealth of the Church, which at the beginning of the 16th century owned over a quarter of all the cultivated land in England. Why, demanded the Vice-Gerent in Spirituals, were monastic orders so rich, when they professed a religion whose Founder had clearly stated that it was easier for a camel to go through the Needle's Eye – a very narrow gate – than for a rich man to enter the Kingdom of Heaven? Something would have to be done about this state of affairs and he, Thomas Cromwell, was the man to do it.

So it was that between the years 1534 and 1540 ecclesiastical foundations up and down the country lived in fear and uncertainty as his appointed commissioners swooped down on their monasteries, listing and valuing all they possessed. As soon as this *Valor Ecclesiasticus* was completed, worse followed as another wave of Cromwell's appointees conducted the most rigorous of visitations to every monastery and convent in England to assess whether their inhabitants were behaving strictly according to the rules of their order.

In many cases, they were not. Cromwell was no admirer of the priesthood, and knew very well that most of the richest monasteries no longer paid even lip-service to their vows of Poverty, Chastity and Obedience.

Where the monks of Tewkesbury were concerned, poverty

had been abandoned years ago, and by the 16th century the Abbey, built near the spot where a simple hermit's cell once stood, had become disgracefully rich.

It had been in 715 that a Saxon lord named Dodo began to build a church in honour of the Virgin Mary near the confluence of the Severn and the smooth-flowing Avon, and ever since, a succession of rich and powerful patrons had added to his original endowment. The church and monks that served there never lacked for funds – indeed, although in Saxon times the church was burned and plundered by Vikings more than once, when resurrected by its next benefactor it was larger and richer than before.

Brictric, King of Wessex, was buried there within the church around the year 800, and in the following century the priory of Tewkesbury became a cell attached to the Benedictine monastery at Cranborne in Dorset. After the Norman Conquest in 1066, another Brictric – whose grandfather Aylward had founded Cranborne Abbey in Dorset in about 980 – was forced to cede both Cranborne and Tewkesbury to the crown. In the medieval equivalent of a reverse takeover, the splendid new church and monastic offices at Tewkesbury built by Robert Fitzhamon, kinsman to William the Conqueror, became the home of the Abbot of Cranborne and his monks, leaving Cranborne itself as a mere dependent cell. Naturally enough, more money and land accrued to Tewkesbury as a result.

The Abbey and monastic buildings took more than half a century to complete. Stone was brought from Caen and transported by barge up the Severn to build the magnificent 148-foot tower. The Abbey's dimensions are almost identical with those of the original Westminster Abbey. It also has the largest external arch in the country, and the sturdy round Norman pillars combine with the delicate Gothic vaulting to breathtaking effect. It is extremely beautiful.

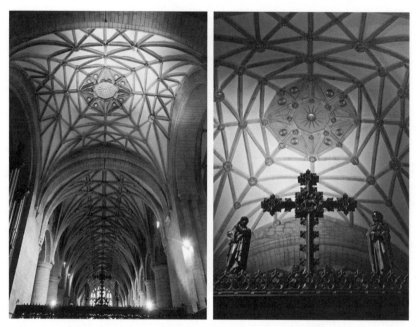

The nave and decorative vaulting of the chancel in Tewkesbury Abbey, showing Edward IV's emblem of 'The Sun in Splendour.'

In the 14th century, when the Black Death ravaged the country, killing about 40% of the population, magnificent tombs and chantries were added around the chancel, built in the perpendicular style which required less manpower, masons then being in short supply. The noble families of Fitzhamon, de Clare, Despenser, Warwick, Beauchamp and Neville are all commemorated there, and from each of these monuments the Abbey benefited significantly.

Situated as it is at the junction of two great rivers, land around the Abbey is susceptible to flooding, but the medieval builders knew all about water-levels, and ensured that the foundations of the Church of St Mary the Virgin raised it above any threat from the Avon breaking its banks.

As a major crossing point between England and Wales, Tewkesbury was always strategically important and the flat land surrounding it has therefore been the scene of major battles. Bloodiest and most decisive was the Yorkist victory in 1471, when Edward IV and his brother Richard, Duke of Gloucester, outflanked the Lancastrian force and drove the nobles back to the steps of the Abbey itself, pursuing them into the nave when they tried to claim sanctuary at the altar. Prince Edward, the Lancastrian heir to the throne, was killed and with him the best hope of a Lancastrian restoration.

Fighting inside a church was the most heinous of crimes. The sanctuary, which had been polluted by the shedding of blood, had to be purified and reconsecrated by the Bishop of Down and Connor, but evidence of the Yorkists' triumph can be detected in the beautifully decorated red-and-white ceiling in the Choir with gilded bosses surrounding the 'Sun in Splendour,' the personal emblem of Edward IV.

Following the battle, Prince Edward of Lancaster was buried at Tewkesbury Abbey and so, later, was George, Duke of Clarence, the thoroughly unreliable Yorkist brother of King Edward IV, who was popularly supposed to have been drowned in a butt of malmsey wine. Clarence's wife Isabel, a great heiress and elder daughter of Warwick the Kingmaker, was buried there too.

Throughout the Middle Ages as royal families rose and fell and kings were crowned or deposed, succeeding Abbots of Tewkesbury continued to amass money and land, appropriating churches from Llandaff to Tarrant Monachorum in Dorset, whenever the opportunity arose. Their appetite was insatiable, though little of what they accrued was spent on hospitality or succouring the needy.

When the Bishop of Worcester made a visitation in 1378 to check on the running of the monastery, he wrote a blistering report on the Abbot's failure to present a yearly statement of accounts to the chapter, castigating him for the poor quality of bread, weak ale, and neglected education of the younger monks. At the time of his visit there had been no hostiller to welcome guests and see to their comfort, no napkins or towels provided for the sick, and no doctor. Worst of all, the bell-tower was in a dangerous condition, and he ordered that repairs should be put in hand at once.

Such hard-hitting reports were rare, however, and in general the Abbots enjoyed almost unfettered freedom to appoint or remove the monastery's officers at will. Most visitations from the see of Worcester were purely formal, and in common with other Benedictine houses, Tewkesbury was managed on a generous scale. Nearly 150 servants were employed to maintain the buildings, farms and gardens, and look after the needs of 40-odd monks. Clothes and education were provided for a number of poor boys and scholars, and the hostiller, cellarer and almoner were responsible for supplies of food and wine for the Abbot's table.

This, then, was the flourishing establishment that came under the cold scrutiny of Thomas Cromwell's commissioners in 1536, and they wasted no time in listing all its valuables and property: manors, boroughs, rents, rectories, relics, tithes, pensions and priories. Rich pickings, indeed, for the Treasury. In January 1540, the Abbot surrendered the monastery and was pensioned off with £266. 13s 4p, though he didn't have to live off this meagre sum for long, since in September the following year he was consecrated to the new see of Gloucester.

The monks were dispersed, their land confiscated. Tapestries, jewels, furniture and plate were loaded on to carts, bound for the Treasury, but when the order came to strip lead from the roof and take down the bells of the Abbey itself, the townspeople of Tewkesbury protested vigorously. The Church of St Mary the Virgin was, they claimed, their own parish church and should not be destroyed, leaving them nowhere to worship. After some brisk negotiation, they carried their point and were permitted to buy their church for £453. 5s. 2d, plus £142 for the eight bells which would otherwise have been melted down and recast as cannons – a deal which must rank as one of the best bargains of all time.

So this former seat of the Benedictine Order became a parish church – albeit an unusually large one – and so it has remained to the present day, serene and beautiful between its two rivers, the only parish church in England to possess two four-manual organs in working order. Of these, the principal – known as the Milton because the author of *Paradise Lost* is said to have played it – was made for Magdalen College, Oxford, and brought to Tewkesbury in 1737. It is regularly used for services, while the Grove, installed during the reign of Queen Victoria, is kept for special recitals.

Tewkesbury Abbey: east view with the High Altar.

Chapter Four

THE FALL OF THE HOUSE OF YORK

Love him or loathe him, the name of the Duke of Gloucester who became King Richard III always evokes strong feelings, and every schoolchild remembers the central mystery of his brief reign long after all the Henrys and Edwards of the Plantagenet dynasty have faded into a blur.

Did he murder the Princes in the Tower? Was he a ruthless, ambitious, misshapen monster or a wise legislator and valiant knight? A child-killer or a loving uncle whose name has been hideously blackened by those who wrested the throne from him?

This most famous Duke of Gloucester was born in 1452, and although his father, Richard of York, was of royal blood and heir presumptive to his cousin King Henry VI, as his eleventh child and fourth son young Richard's own chances of ascending the throne looked very slim. It was another matter for his father, who had both a good claim and a pack of ambitious sons eager to fight for the crown. When the weak, pious, inept Henry VI, who had managed to lose most of the French territory won by his father at the battle of Agincourt, lost his wits as well, the Yorkist branch of the family combined with the powerful Earl of Warwick, 'the Kingmaker,' to launch their bid for control of the kingdom.

So began what came to be called the Wars of the Roses – red for the House of Lancaster (Henry VI's supporters) and white for the House of York. Back and forth across the country the battles raged. When Richard of York together with his eldest son Edmund was killed at Wakefield, his glamorous second son Edward, six foot four at the age of nineteen and a brilliant tactician, took up the family claim to the throne. Meanwhile his young brothers George and Richard remained in the safety of the Low Countries until, upon Edward's eventual victory over the Lancastrian forces and coronation in 1471, he created the 14-year-old George Duke of Clarence, and Richard, aged eleven, Duke of Gloucester.

Throughout his teens, Richard proved a doughty fighter, though in looks the three brothers were quite unlike. Edward was handsome, big, blond and boisterous, George – who had been his mother's favourite – had a look of permanent discontent, while Richard, who took after his father, was sharp-featured, small, dark and wiry, with a shrewd legalistic mind and a distinctly puritan streak in his character. No contemporary mention was made of a hunchback or withered arm – that may have been a Tudor invention – though overdeveloped muscles in his sword arm could well have made one shoulder look higher than the other.

So different were the brothers in appearance, in fact, that scurrilous rumours circulated that Edward's real father might have been an archer named Blaybourne or Blackburn, though no one could produce any evidence beyond his looks and keen eye for the ladies. Far too keen an eye. It led to a lot of trouble. In fact, if King Edward IV, as he became after the decisive battles of Towton and Tewkesbury in 1461, could have resisted the impulse to propose marriage to more than one lady at a time, English history might well have taken a different course.

Unfortunately he didn't. Not content with romantic liaisons

with a string of Court beauties which resulted in a brood of bastard children, he infuriated his powerful cousin Warwick the Kingmaker by secretly marrying a beautiful but extremely grasping widow, Elizabeth Woodville, whose large family were Lancastrian sympathisers. No sooner was she crowned Queen, that she began to shoehorn her brothers into important and lucrative official positions, and arrange noble marriages for her female relations. She herself was notably fertile, producing ten children with the King as well as two sons from her first marriage.

Since his Queen was almost continuously pregnant, Edward carried on disporting himself with court beauties and merchants' wives – he wasn't choosy – often sharing his mistresses with friends in his liberal, open-handed way. Lively, witty Jane Shore, whom he described as his 'merriest whore', was passed on to Lord Hastings, who later had reason to regret this mark of royal favour, while yet another of her lovers was the Queen's eldest son from her first marriage, who had now become the Earl of Dorset.

Richard married once only, but this alliance brought him a great power base in the north. Rather as modern boys are often despatched to prep school at the age of eight or nine, in medieval days sons of noble families would be placed in the household of a powerful relation who would supervise their education and teach them their knightly duties. These were many and varied, ranging from serving their lord at table, elements of falconry, hunting etiquette, tilting and jousting as well as the serious use of weapons, to more sedentary pursuits such as learning their family tree by heart, playing musical instruments and acquiring as much Latin as the strong arm of the resident priest could beat into them.

It was at Middleham Castle in Yorkshire, in the household of his cousin Warwick the Kingmaker, that Richard acquired his knightly training, and there he passed what were probably the happiest years of his childhood, in the company of other boys including his lifelong friend Francis Lovell, and Warwick's

True to his motto, 'Loyalty Binds Me,' Richard, Duke of Gloucester faithfully supported his brother King Edward IV. Would he then, as King Richard III, have ordered the murder of Edward's sons? The charge remains unproven.

daughters Isabella and Anne Neville. After the Kingmaker's death it was Anne whom Richard married, and from Middleham that he watched with disapproval the elevation of the Queen's greedy ambitious kinsmen.

Still he remained loyal to his brother. How could he do otherwise, with his personal motto, *Loyaulté me lie* – Loyalty Binds Me – boldly emblazoned above the white boars supporting his coat of arms?

Loyalty continued to bind him throughout his brother's reign. Unlike his sibling the Duke of Clarence, Richard of Gloucester could not be tempted to join in the sporadic rebellions of the next ten years. Appointed Governor of the North, he was the King's most powerful and trusted lieutenant, and was widely respected for his integrity and insistence on justice for all.

Hard-living, hard-loving King Edward IV died unexpectedly after falling into the water while salmon-fishing and catching a feverish chill. He was only 40 and his recently pacified kingdom was quite unprepared for the danger of minority rule. Like a shaken kaleidoscope, patterns of behaviour and relationships changed abruptly as the greatest nobles in the realm repositioned themselves for personal advantage.

By the late King's will, Richard was appointed as Lord Protector of his young sons and, having good reason to fear the influence of the Queen's family, he raised a strong force of Yorkshiremen and hurried from Middleham to intercept her brother Lord Rivers as he escorted the young king from Ludlow towards London to be crowned.

The two parties met at Stony Stratford. When Rivers proved reluctant to give up his charge, Richard had him arrested, and himself conducted the future Edward V the rest of the way to his capital. Londoners, suspicious of armed Yorkshiremen, gave them only a cautious welcome and the Queen, true to form, gathered up all the treasures she could lay hands on before retiring with the rest of her children to sanctuary in Westminster.

On the advice of Lord Hastings the young king was lodged in the Royal Apartments at the Tower of London to await his coronation on June 22nd.

For the next two months preparations went forward under Richard's supervision, but just a fortnight before the coronation the kaleidoscope was shaken again, and as the pieces settled the picture they now formed was murky. In a meeting of the Parliamentary lords on June 9th, the Bishop of Bath and Wells, Robert Stillington, made the shocking allegation that, before his secret marriage to Elizabeth Woodville, King Edward had contracted to marry yet another pretty widow, Lady Eleanor Talbot – during the Wars of the Roses, widows were thick on the ground.

A pre-contract of marriage was a serious matter in those days, as legally binding as marriage itself, and if the Bishop's revelation was true, it meant that Edward IV was a bigamist, all his offspring with Elizabeth Woodville were illegitimate, and young Edward V had no right to the throne of England.

Was Stillington's accusation true? Since no records survive of that crucial Parliamentary meeting, one can only guess. He was a thoroughly worldly priest, deeply involved in politics, and during Edward IV's reign he had already served one stint in prison for treasonous conspiracy with Edward's disaffected brother George, Duke of Clarence. For that crime, George had been attainted by the Commons, and privately executed in the Tower, though the terms of the charges against him remained vague. Slandering the king. Conspiracy. High treason. Could it be that Stillington had told him about the pre-contract with Eleanor Talbot, and George had attempted to blackmail the King with his knowledge?

Only when Edward was safely dead did Stillington bring the matter to the attention of the Parliamentary lords, giving them no choice but to declare Edward's children by Elizabeth Woodville illegitimate.

Though abrupt reversals of fortune were by no means uncommon in the 15th century, this one must have been particularly disorientating for the boy-king in the Tower. One day he was being measured for his coronation robes. The next he had become the Lord Bastard, and his hopes of the throne were gone. Nevertheless, he now had the consolation of a playfellow to cheer his solitude since the Queen had agreed to let his younger brother Richard join him in the Tower, and for the next two months the boys were seen from time to time, playing with a ball in the grounds of the White Tower.

Then, in August 1483, they vanished – and no one has ever been sure what became of them.

Theories abounded, then and now, but before considering in whose interest it would have been to have them disposed of, it is necessary to examine the events of that crucial month which culminated in the coronation of King Richard III.

Bishop Stillington's revelation of the pre-contract was on June 9th, and at once the court split between those who believed him and the sceptics who remained committed to the boy-king's cause. Foremost among the latter was Baron Hastings, the late King Edward's boon companion, who had inherited his mistress Jane Shore and was not now going to desert Edward's son.

Four days later, on June 13th, in the Council chamber, Richard made a dramatic accusation of witchcraft against Jane Shore and the former Queen. Their spells, he claimed, had bewitched his sword arm, and as proof he rolled up his sleeve to show its withered appearance. When Hastings began to protest, he was immediately arrested and executed without trial – a very black mark against Richard.

It is curious, however, that Jane Shore, against whom the accusation was made and who might have been expected to share Hastings's fate or at least be subjected to one of the horrible medieval trials for witchcraft, was merely ordered to do penance by parading through the City barefoot, in her shift. Since she was very pretty and well-liked, an ad hoc guard of chivalrous well-wishers protected her from the rougher elements in the crowd come to witness her punishment, and this mild penance contrasts so sharply with the barbarous treatment meted out to Hastings that one can't help suspecting the witchcraft accusation was really an excuse to get rid of him. He was hand-in-glove with another of Jane Shore's former lovers, Lord Dorset, himself the Queen's eldest son, and the four of them formed a power block opposed to Richard and likely to cause trouble.

More heads rolled on the 25th June, when the boy king's uncle and ex-guardian Lord Rivers, and Richard Grey, second son of the Queen's first marriage, were executed at Pontefract.

On the very same day in London, Parliament presented a petition to Richard on behalf of the Three Estates – the Lords spiritual and temporal, and the Commons – known as *Titulus Regius*, the Title of King.

Addressed to 'The High and Mighty Prince, Richard Duc of Gloucester', the petition began by sorrowfully listing the troubles and afflictions that had befallen the once-tranquil and prosperous kingdom during the 'ungracious pretensed marriage' of the late King Edward IV, which 'was made of grete presumption, without the knowyng or assent of the lords of this londe; and also by sorcerie and wich-craft, committed by the said Elizabeth Grey and her moder...'

This was not the first time that the former Queen and her mother had been suspected of witchcraft : one of the accusations against Jane Shore was that she had dabbled in magic in association with Queen Elizabeth.

Next *Titulus Regius* outlined the reasons why Richard was now the only possible Yorkist candidate for the throne. Since his brother Edward had been bigamously married, his children were ineligible. Likewise George, Duke of Clarence, who would have been next in line, had been executed as a traitor, and his sons were attainted. So who did that leave? None other than Richard, Duke of Gloucester, might 'by right... clayme the said coroune and dignitie roiall by way of enheritaunce...'

Despite the courtly exaggeration and sycophantic tone of the following passages heaping praise on his 'greate prudence, justice, princely courage and excellent virtue,' it is clear that at that point Richard was esteemed and respected, and the Three Estates expressed confidence that his accession to the throne would deliver them from the 'thraldom and bondage as we have lyved long tyme heretofore, oppressed and injured by new extorcos and imposicons against the law of God and man...'

No hint there of any worries or rumours that he had murdered his nephews; but when, after the Commons had given their assent to this Bill and Richard, having put on a diplomatic show of reluctance, agreed to accept the crown on the 6th July, it was not long before the gossipmongers were out in force. While the new king set out on a royal progress through the Midlands to Gloucester, insidious whispers began to circulate.

Where were the young princes? they asked. Why were they no longer seen playing in the gardens of the White Tower? Had they been spirited away to France? To the Low Countries? Were they alive or dead?

Presently the rumours crystallised into direct accusations against their uncle. The States-General of France were told unequivocally that Richard had ordered the murder of his nephews. They had been smothered as they slept, and their bodies buried under a staircase which was being rebuilt in the Tower. Their killers had even been identified as Sir James Tyrell, a long-term supporter of Richard's, and his henchmen John Dighton and Miles Forest.

Whether or not the new king was aware of the rumours, he did nothing to silence them. Admittedly, he had plenty else to worry about. The Duke of Buckingham, who had always been his close ally, loaded with lands and honours and created Constable of England, had now rebelled and joined forces with Henry Tudor, Earl of Richmond, to challenge Richard for the crown.

Henry Tudor's claim to the throne was tenuous, to say the least. Descended from Henry V's Queen and her second husband, Owen Tudor, his early life had been spent in Wales and France under the guardianship of his uncle Jasper Tudor, awaiting an opportunity to launch his own effort to bring down the House of York.

He had chosen a very dangerous ally. Buckingham was himself a Plantagenet, royally descended on both his father and mother's sides. He had, indeed, a better claim to the throne than Henry Tudor himself. Buckingham raised a large army in Wales and, in the autumn of 1483, marched towards England, meaning to join forces with the Breton contingent which the King of France, ever keen to stir the pot of English discord, had recruited for him.

It had been a miserable wet summer, and in the autumn the rain never stopped. Livestock drowned in their flooded fields, crops rotted, and when Buckingham's army reached the Severn, they found to their dismay that the river had burst its banks, making the crossing impossible. Richmond, meanwhile, was storm-bound in Brittany, unable to leave harbour.

Cold, wet and disheartened, Buckingham's troops deserted him. His rebellion was over without a blow being struck, and although he sought refuge with a supporter, he was soon betrayed, taken captive and, although he tried to talk his way out of trouble by evoking their earlier friendship, Richard coldly refused to meet him before he, too, was executed.

The first and only Parliament of Richard's reign dealt with a number of pressing legal matters. The system of bail which still operates today was introduced by him, as was the standardisation of weights and measures. During his reign he abolished Benevolences, or forced loans, and did away with the discreditable system by which rich men could purchase high office instead of achieving it by merit. He also took the important step of making English, rather than Latin or French, the language of law.

Nevertheless, like a smouldering peat fire that bursts into new flames whenever an earlier conflagration is extinguished, rebellions continued to break out. Warwick, Buckingham, and Clarence were dead, along with many of the Queen's most overtly ambitious male relations, but the ever-persistent Henry Tudor, Earl of Richmond and his scheming mother, now married to Lord Stanley, still posed a real danger, and two heavy blows further undermined Richard's position.

First his only legitimate son, Edward of Middleham, Prince of Wales, fell into a consumptive decline and died, followed a few months later by his mother Anne, the Queen. The tragedy of losing his small family was compounded for Richard by character assassination: rumours that he had poisoned the Queen in order to clear the way to marry his lively niece Elizabeth of York, elder sister of the young princes, began to spread until he was forced to deny them publicly, and send his niece away from Court.

Another wet summer. Another invasion. Again in 1485 Richmond, now backed by his uncle Jasper Tudor, landed at Milford Haven with an army of French mercenaries, and marched towards London. King Richard was at Nottingham, and hurried south to intercept his challenger, but many of his allies hesitated before committing themselves to his service.

Rumour and counter-rumour spread across the country; spies were planted in every noble household, and intelligence agents scurried to and fro bearing cryptic messages. *Jockey of Norfolk, be not too bold, For Dickon thy master is bought and sold,* one warned John ('Jockey') Howard, but it was advice the loyal Duke of Norfolk chose to ignore – with fatal results.

On a sultry day in late August, the armies faced each other on the low-lying, swampy ground to the south of Market Bosworth in Leicestershire.

Richard had more troops – 5000 against 3000 – but he knew their loyalty was far from assured. The large contingent commanded by Lord Stanley, in particular, could not be relied on, since his wife was Richmond's mother. Prudently, Richard took the precaution of arresting Stanley's son Lord Strange as a hostage, hoping thereby to ensure that Stanley's men fought on the right side, but when in the first wave of fighting the vanguard commanded by Norfolk was overwhelmed, Stanley's force remained immobile on the hill above, while the Duke of Northumberland also held back, waiting to see who was likely to win.

Infuriated by their treachery, Richard ordered the immediate execution of Lord Strange, but his command was not obeyed. There was nothing for it but to hurl his own bodyguard into the fray, seeking his enemy beneath the fluttering red dragon of the Tudors.

Conspicuous on his favourite charger White Surrey, and still wearing the crown, he unhorsed the jousting champion Sir John Cheney, and cut down Sir William Brandon, Richmond's massive standard-bearer, before his horse became bogged in the swampy ground. Richard continued the fight on foot and was within yards of Henry Tudor himself when Lord Stanley at last ordered his men forward for the kill.

Alone and surrounded by foes, but still 'fighting manfully in the thickest press of his enemies,' according to the Tudor historian Polydore Vergil, Richard was finally stabbed to death, the last English king to die in battle, and the crown rolled away beneath a hawthorn bush.

So ended the Plantagenet line of kings, and the victorious Henry Tudor, crowned as Henry VII, took good care that it could never return. His own claim to the throne being decidedly shaky, he was quick to marry Elizabeth of York, sister of the Princes in the Tower, and to order the destruction of all copies of *Titulus Regius* which had proclaimed her illegitimate. He issued a proclamation accusing Richard of cruelty and tyranny but this, strangely, made no mention of the missing princes.

Then, and throughout his reign, he was keenly alive to the threat from possible Yorkist heirs or pretenders. Not only from Lambert Simnel and Perkin Warbeck, each of whom claimed to be the younger of the missing princes, but Richard's bastard son, and the mentally deficient Edward Plantagenet, earl of Warwick, 'who couldn't tell a goose from a capon', were ruthlessly disposed of. Even old Margaret de la Pole, Countess of Salisbury, was executed at the age of 78 for the sin of having Yorkist blood.

Yet in the household accounts of Middleham Castle, Richard III's stronghold, there are references to expenses incurred in feeding and clothing two unidentified boys during Richard's short reign. Could he have hidden the missing princes there, fearing for their safety in the Tower? Could they, indeed, have survived until after Richard's death in battle, only to be secretly killed later by order of Henry VII?

For it is not until July 1486, a year *after* the Battle of Bosworth, that the murder charge is officially laid at Richard's door by Tudor propagandists. Before that, their disappearance is presented as a rumour. After 1486 it becomes accepted fact.

Nearly two hundred years later, in the reign of Charles II, the skeletons of two children were discovered in a chest during the demolition of a staircase leading to the chapel in the White Tower. Scraps of velvet and silk hung about the bones, indicating that they were of high status. Examination revealed them to belong to children of approximately the age of the missing princes, though it was impossible to determine their gender. The elder child's jawbone provided evidence of disease, while the younger's jaw was missing.

Location, era, victims – all neatly fitted the rumour put about by Richard's enemies in 1484. Too neatly? Could the princes, hidden at Middleham during their uncle's reign, have been brought back to the Tower and there murdered a year later in order to make the rumour true?

It is an inescapable fact that they went missing on Richard's watch, when they were under his protection, but it is not inconceivable that a loyal, loving uncle might have seen the danger they posed – not to him – but to other claimants to the throne, and decided to keep them out of harm's way until they could fend for themselves. After all, Richard himself had spent much of his childhood in hiding from his brother's many enemies.

The skeletons in the chest may well have been those of the missing princes. The question is: who put them there? The rebellious Duke of Buckingham? Or Henry VII himself, who had such a track record in disposing of Yorkist heirs.

Though Richard III himself will always be the prime suspect, not least because of Shakespeare's efforts in depicting him as a monster, such a secret, hole-and-corner murder of his defenceless nephews seems strangely out of character for a man who either slew his enemies in battle or publicly ordered their execution – then took care to protect their widows and children.

Loyaulté me lie was his personal motto, and throughout his life his loyalty to his family was beyond question. Would he have been complicit in the secret murder of his brother's children?

Amid the shifting sand of speculation, only one thing is certain. At this distance in time, no one will ever know for sure.

Chapter Five

THE BISLEY BOY

Why did Queen Elizabeth I never marry? What was the mysterious physical defect which, according to contemporary Tudor gossip, debarred her from matrimony?

Gloucestershire has many royal connections. In our own time, both Prince Charles and his sister the Princess Royal have homes in the county, and throughout history stories have been told of the kings and queens who have fought and dwelt, been crowned and died in the Cotswolds. There can, however, be few more bizarre than the legend of the Bisley Boy.

The small village of Bisley lies in a fold of the high Cotswold ridge, a few miles from the bustling market town of Stroud. In Tudor days Over Court was a royal hunting lodge and, so the story goes, Princess Elizabeth was sent there in 1542 to avoid the plague which was raging through the narrow, overcrowded streets of London. She was then nine years old, and since the birth of her brother Edward, no longer the sole Protestant heir to King Henry VIII's throne. Her elder sister, Mary, who clung stubbornly to Catholicism, had been declared illegitimate and barred from the succession.

Bisley may have seemed a healthy spot, but it was not far enough to escape contagion, and by ill luck – so the story goes

– Princess Elizabeth succumbed to a fever while she was there, and died a few days later, just when her household learned to their horror that the King himself planned to visit Over Court on his way to hunt from Berkeley Castle.

Prince Edward was a sickly child but, so delighted was he to have a male heir at last, the King had paid little attention to Elizabeth during the past five years and seldom saw her. He was renowned for his hasty temper and the violence of his rages, and no one in the Princess's household dared to give him the terrible news of her death.

Instead, according to the legend, they buried her hastily and searched neighbouring villages for a child resembling her whom they could formally present to the King.

No red-headed girl of roughly the right age could be found, and they were forced into the desperate expedient of substituting

St Mary's Church, Bisley: does its graveyard contain the secret?

one of her playmates, a white-faced, delicate-featured, carrot-topped boy of fourteen, and coaching him to play the part of the Princess. Some say he was a village lad, but others maintain he was a bastard son of Henry's own, which would have accounted for the resemblance.

Carefully rehearsed, the boy performed well, causing Henry to pronounce him a comely lass, well versed in Greek and Latin, 'a wise head on young shoulders'.

Off cantered the King and his hunting party, and the Princess's household heaved a sigh of relief – or at least they did until they realised that now they were stuck with the deception. They could neither admit the masquerade nor reverse it. From now on the Bisley Boy must play the Princess until an opportunity arose to dispose of him.

Time passed. Henry VIII himself died, and at the age of ten the sickly Prince became King Edward VI. The substitute Princess Elizabeth moved a step nearer the throne, and came under more intense public scrutiny. There was no chance to get rid of the Bisley Boy with so many eyes watching the Princess's every move.

Six years later Edward died, probably from a combination of tuberculosis and measles, and after a power struggle his rejected elder sister was crowned as Queen Mary: 'Bloody Mary,' as she is known to history, for the multitude of deaths she caused in wrenching the country back to Roman Catholicism.

She even sent her sister Princess Elizabeth to the Tower of London where, when she fell ill, she is recorded as saying, 'I am not minded to make any stranger privy to my body, but commit it to the will of God.' In other words, no messing about or examination by strange medicoes who would inevitably discover her secret.

The same interdiction extended to a postmortem examination after her death in 1603. Or was it *his* death? Could any man have kept up the deception so successfully or so long?

Five years after becoming queen, Mary died following a phantom pregnancy, and Elizabeth succeeded to the throne to begin the long and glorious reign in which she adroitly avoided marrying any of her many suitors, blowing hot and cold by turns on the kings and courtiers who pursued her, determined at all costs to avoid plunging the country back into religious strife and steadfastly to remain her own woman. Or man.

Consider the passage from her famous speech to her troops at Tilbury at the time of the Spanish Armada, when she declared: 'I know I have the body of a weak and feeble woman, but I have the heart and stomach of a King.' Consider the masculinity of her mind and temperament compared to the intense femininity of her cousin Mary, Queen of Scots. Men fell head over heels in love

The graveyard at St Mary's Bisley, where the Tudor child was allegedly re-buried.

with Mary, but Elizabeth, with her bald pate, thick white make-up and extravagant glittering dresses, was treated with caution by all her suitors.

There are a host of reasons that make the boy-into-girl story impossible. Shaving. Puberty. Voice. The sheer difficulty of concealing so basic a difference in the long term. Yet in the village of Bisley's spring festival for over three hundred years the part of the Queen of the May was always played by a boy in Tudor costume.

However the follow-up story that, during renovations at Over Court in the 1860s, the vicar of Bisley, the serious-minded Rev Thomas Keble, told his family that he had secretly reburied the remains of a girl aged about nine, dressed in Tudor clothes, which he had found in a stone coffin, is probably a joke invented by his son. Certainly no one else has ever discovered it.

Chapter Six

THE GOLDEN FLEECE

Central to the attractions of Gloucestershire in the eyes of Romans, Saxons, Normans, and all the other landowners who followed was its high, open limestone grassland – the perfect place to rear sheep and produce wool.

Shivering in tunics and togas, the Southern Europeans who had made themselves masters of the fairest places on earth quickly realised that to survive the fogs, frosts and rains of an English winter in reasonable comfort, they needed much warmer clothing.

At that time the native sheep were what we now call Primitives, with no more than a covering of 'kemp' or coarse, crinkly hair which they shed naturally in summer, as a horse or cow does. It is too short to spin or weave, and therefore need not be shorn. The only British fleece-shedding breed that survives in any numbers today is the Wiltshire Horn, and since wool is no longer regarded as a valuable commodity – it costs more to shear a flock than the farmer can recoup by selling the fleeces – this lack of a proper fleece is regarded as an advantage. In recent years attempts have been made to cross Wiltshire Horns with other breeds so that they, too, may in effect shear themselves. Australians have even experimented with hormones that cause the sheep's fleece to rise up from the skin and fall off, a process known as bio-shearing.

It was very different in Roman times. According to the historian Tacitus, an extensive clothing trade existed at Cirencester early in the first century of the Christian era. In those days, wool was highly valued: warm, light and even, if the natural lanolin was not washed out of it, semi-weatherproof. To improve the quality, Romans may well have imported rams from long-woolled Italian breeds such as the Turchessa, renowned for the softness of its fleece, or the Altamurana, whose curls hang down to knee-level, to cross with the native Primitives. Whatever mixture of genes was used, the result was the making of Gloucestershire's most reliable moneyspinner for the next fifteen hundred years – the sheep on whose 'golden fleeces' the county's economy depended, which came to be known affectionately as the 'Cotswold Lions.'

In appearance these are tall, rangy, big-boned animals, white all over and standing almost waist-high to a human, with a bold, alert expression and delicate, wide-set ears. 'Long-backed and square of bulk and bone,' was one Elizabethan description, while in the 14th song of his *Poly-Olbion*, published in 1614, Michael Drayton waxes lyrical about their pure whiteness, with 'no black or brown on legs or face; the brows woolly, and the flank as well covered as the back; the staple deep and thick; the body long and large.' They have no horns, and one of their most easily identified characteristics is the length of the corkscrew curls that cover them all over, right down to the fetlock, and flop attractively over their brows.

Opinion differed over the quality of the wool. In a fourteenth-century treatise for merchants, *La Practica della Mercatura*, Cotswold wool was valued at 11 marks (roughly £8) per sack, with each sack containing about 150 fleeces, which was considerably less than the 28 marks per sack Lombard merchants would pay for the highest quality wool from Monmouthshire and Herefordshire.

In *The Shepherd's Sure Guide,* by William Ellis, published in 1749, he declares that *'on those famous hills called Cotswold Hills, sheep are fed that produce a singular good wool, which for Fineness comes very near to that of Spain; for from it a thread may be drawn as fine as silk.'*

Only thirty years later, however, another writer described the fleece as 'prodigious but coarse... so that the Cotswold wool which was never fine within the memory of any man I have conversed with on that subject, is now become still coarser.'

The truth may lie somewhere between the two. Probably the well-fed, carefully-bred Cotswold sheep belonging to monasteries had superior fleeces to the hard-living flocks grazing on bleak upland pastures of the open-field system, which grew as much wool as they needed for warmth, and never mind the quality. Indeed, so thick, heavy and curly is the Cotswold fleece

Shearing was always backbreaking work, even after the invention of power-driven clippers like this early Lister model.

that the thought of shearing even one with hand-blades is enough to make an amateur shepherd quail.

Yet shorn by hand they were, in their tens of thousands, every year from Roman times until the invention of power-driven clippers in the 1880s. Since the world record for blade-shearing which was set in 1892 is still 321 sheep in 7 hours and 40 minutes, while the record using electric clippers stands at 720 in 9 hours, with several sheep shorn in 38 seconds flat, it demonstrates just how strong and skilful shearers were in days of yore, and how much time it must have taken to produce the raw material of Gloucestershire's wealth.

The shepherd's year was a busy one, with little time for leisurely dalliance with flounce-skirted, bonnet-wearing damsels or idle playing of the flute as shepherds are so often depicted in porcelain statuettes, or in idyllic poems and paintings of pastoral life. On the contrary, his work was labour-intensive and lonely, best suited to men who preferred the silent company of their sheepdogs to the hurly-burly of a family home.

Right through the annual shepherding cycle dogs and men were kept hard at work. Their year began in autumn, when the rams would be put in with the ewes, traditionally on November 5th, so that the lambs might be expected from April Fool's Day onward, when spring grass had begun to grow. When tupping was over and the sexes separated once more, the harsh weather would force the flocks down from the high pastures and kickstart the flockmaster's winter schedule, with its heavy demands for extra feeding and vigilance against predators, by no means all of whom had four legs.

Sheep-stealing was a common crime, despite the severity of the punishment meted out to offenders regardless of their age or the degree of desperation which had forced them to risk abstracting a fat ewe or lamb from the huge, tempting flocks so close at hand. Children of eight would be condemned to hang

along with their elders for stealing sheep or, after the establishment of penal colonies on the far side of the world, sentenced to
the hardly less horrible fate of transportation to America or later,
after the American War of Independence, the grim, unfamiliar
shores of Australia and Tasmania.

Even more gruesome in our eyes was the relish with which
our forebears abandoned their work and flocked in excited bands
to watch a public hanging, but in an age with little in the way of
entertainment, their pleasure in the break from routine toil made
the occasion as good as a holiday.

In his diary for April 28th, 1827, the country parson the Rev.
F.E. Witts records that *As we went towards Cheltenham, we marvelled
at the crowds of people of the lower orders trudging on towards Gloucester,
with great eagerness, young and middle-aged, and many females. We
knew not of any Fair or race or merry meeting: at last the truth flashed on
my recollection, all these people were hurrying to witness the execution of
the wretched brothers Dyer who are to expiate their crimes this morning
by their deaths...*

When the malefactors had been exhibited to one and all and
allowed to proclaim a few last words, the noose would be adjusted
about their necks, the cart they were standing on driven away,
and the thieves left to struggle unsupported until they choked to
death. Later the corpses would be buried at some bleak crossroads
which might thereafter bear an identifying name, such as Shipton's
Grave, near Tetbury, where a sheep-stealer was interred with a
stake of elder through his heart.

It is said that on one occasion, at least, a would-be sheep-
stealer was throttled by the fat ewe he was carrying by means of
a rope slung round his own neck. Pausing to rest his burden on
a handy stone post by the roadside, he failed to centre it on the
support. The heavy carcase slipped, and the rope round his gullet
did the rest. Since this cautionary tale, with variations, occurs all
over the county, it was probably promoted and embellished as a

message to anyone tempted to steal a sheep that if the law didn't catch you, fate would make sure you did not profit from your crime.

Having brought his flocks through the winter, a shepherd's next drama was the lambing, which often results in complications: problems of surplus or orphaned lambs demanding hand-rearing or elaborate adoption schemes, the disposal of carcases, identification of singles, twins and triplets, then tailing and castrating, amid a barrage of baa-ing and bleating which never ceases day or night. Like many animals whose principal defence is flight, ewes naturally time their moment of giving birth to the darkest hours when they are most likely to escape unwelcome notice, which means many broken nights for the supervising shepherd, anxious to be on hand to assist if needed.

The Market House or Tolsey in Tetbury was built in 1655 and after hundreds of years as a noted centre for the wool trade is still in regular use by local traders.

April has always been a fraught month for the shepherd in the Cotswolds, as he watches his flock more than double in size while the spring grass remains stubbornly reluctant to grow; but May brings a brief respite, with warmer weather and a sudden spurt of growth that covers the high, brashy plateau with a carpet of green. That was when the great flocks of 'Cotswold Lions' would leave the valleys where they had wintered and manured the lower fields of the village, and spread out across the high sheepwalks in a hungry tide.

Under the open-field system of pasturage where each flock was allotted grazing rights in particular areas, the sheep would be led out to from their wattle-hurdle folds early in the morning, kept together by the constant vigilance of the shepherd and his dogs, and be brought back to the safety of the folds at night.

The construction of wattle hurdles was an industry in itself, with gangs of old men and young boys kept constantly employed in weaving the basket-like fencing in six-foot long, four-foot high sections with loops to secure them at the corners.

Keeping the steadily-munching jaws of those Cotswold Lions well filled was always a juggling act. Ploughland belonged either to freeholders, or to the Lord of the Manor, who leased it to tenant farmers by the 'yardland,' a measure of land of uncertain quantity varying from fifteen to forty acres according to its quality, productivity, and position in the country. Other pasture was leased by the virgate, but this, too, was complicated, since a virgate was equal to two bovates or one-eighth of a carucate. There were either twelve or eighteen carucates to the hide, which was commonly about 120 acres. Given the flexibility of these measurements, it is not surprising that arguments often arose over the exact dimensions of a tenant's entitlement. Leases for lives dated from about the 16th century, and for lives or 99 years from the 17th century. The 'lives' had to be specified in the lease – usually contracted for father and son. If it extended to a grandson, and when two of the lives had died, it was usual to grant a new lease to the survivor and two new lives.

There was, however, no ambiguity about tithes. Not only did the great monastic foundations of Gloucestershire own many manors, but even after the Dissolution of the Monasteries in 1536, the church continued to claim one-tenth of the agricultural produce of every family in the parish for the support of the priest.

The Midsummer and Martinmas (11th November) tithes were single levies made on wool, lamb, geese, calves, and sometimes pigs. The wool was assessed on the basis of sheep numbers or fleeces, which were classed as Fine, Common, and Wethers. Easter dues were assessed on a variety of produce ranging from horses to honey, and including vegetables, eggs and chicks, and corn and hay.

J. Arthur Gibbs quotes in '*A Cotswold Village*' 'an ancient manuscript which the vicar of Bibury lately acquired, and which contains the history of his parish since the Conquest, are set down some interesting and amusing details concerning tithe and the cash compensations that had been paid time out of mind...

> *For every new Milch cow three pence*
> *For every thorough Milch cow one penny*
> *For every calf weaned a half penny*
> *For every calf sold four pence or the left shoulder*
> *For every calf killed in the family four pence or the left shoulder*
> *Tithe in kind must be paid for all fatting cattle...*

He also recounts how the vicar's man 'went out into the cornfields and placed a bough in every tenth stook of corn. Then the titheman came with the parson's horses and took the stuff away to the tithe barn. The tithe for every cock in the farmyard was three eggs; for every hen, two eggs. Besides poultry, pigs, geese and sheep. The parson had a right to his share of the milk, and even of the cheeses that were made in his parish.' (These

Basket-weavers and other artisans still use the cloistered ground floor area of Tetbury's Market House.

particular tithes, which were levied on produce only, evidently referred to poultry bred in that year.)

No wonder tithes were detested! Like death and taxes, there was no escape from them.

It was the tenant farmer who had to worry about tithes on his sheep. The shepherd's concerns were more directly connected to their welfare. As the weather grew warmer and parasitic insects proliferated, the next major ritual in the year's work was cleaning the animals' valuable fleeces by driving the entire flock through water deep enough to immerse them completely.

'Washpool' and 'Sheepwash' are names that recur in most Cotswold villages. Farmers in the village would organise a rota, and on the appointed day, when the sun was well risen and dew gone from the grass, a white torrent of sheep would flow through the streets, jostling and bleating, each separate flock with its shepherd leading them down to the water and a posse of dogs trotting quietly behind, ever alert to deflect breakaways and encourage stragglers as the flock made its way to the washpool.

This was a time when village boys could make themselves useful, blocking side streets, protecting gardens and shops, or frustrating the efforts of independent-minded animals to go in the wrong direction. Even in my childhood it used to be mandatory for anyone who found their way blocked by an oncoming flock to greet them with the correct date: 'Good morning, sheep. It is... um...' then would follow a long pause as one tried to remember what day it happened to be... 'Thursday, the nineteenth of June, nineteen hundred and forty-eight.' If you managed to get the words out before the first sheep squeezed past, you would be allowed a wish.

Dipping was a noisy, splashy, tumultuous business. Once the leading sheep had been forced down a ramp in single file and into a narrow channel through the water, the village gaffers leaning over the stream would use their long, T-shaped staves to push each animal under long enough to ensure that the whole fleece was thoroughly soaked. The running water would dislodge and float away the ticks and seeds of grass, gorse prickles and other detritus that had collected in the thick, curling wool, and soften the dung-caked 'dags' round the hindquarters. Once the whole flock was washed and dried off in sun and wind, they would be ready to shear.

Again, this was a co-operative effort, with a gang of expert shearers and their assistants moving from farm to farm, steadily working through one flock after the other. The sheep would be penned in a large enclosure, from which small groups would be driven through a narrow race, at the end of which each in turn would be caught by a couple of farm lads and pulled forward to the carefully-swept shearing area. There three or four men might be working simultaneously, vying with one another to clip the fastest.

With the continual bleating of the sheep, shouts and curses of the men chivvying and catching, and the constant *zing-zing, zang-zang* of whetstone on metal, as a cutting edge was put on the shears, it was a noisy, tense occasion, but there was order in the apparent chaos. Each man knew his job and stuck to it as long as daylight lasted for, then as now, in England no one can guarantee fine weather two days in succession, and wet sheep are impossible to shear.

Slowly the density of the unshorn flock would diminish in the collecting pen. As each snowy-skinned, strangely shrunken-looking sheep was released and staggered to its feet again, a 'skirter' would quickly sweep away dirty or unusable wool, leaving the floor clear for the next animal, while the fleece itself would be seized by one of the 'rollers,' neatly folded and compressed into a tight bundle, and stuffed into the one of the big square woolsacks hanging from a beam.

It was hard, demanding work, whose conclusion was always marked with a celebration. After the village's flocks had all been shorn, the shearers' feast would be a splendid occasion, with plenty of food provided by the farmers' wives, lavish cider and beer, and singing that continued far into the night.

Echoes of those shearers' feasts survive even today, when Tetbury holds its traditional Woolsack Races on Whit Monday. Competitors race up, down, or up-and-down the steep hill that used to lead to the livestock market, carrying on their shoulders a 60lb, traditionally shaped woolsack – although in medieval times the sacks were much heavier and wool was far too precious a commodity to be used for this kind of larking about.

Instead, the bulging sacks would be collected by 'broggers' – middlemen – who kept them safely stored in warehouses until the next wool market that merchants from Flanders were expected to attend. There they would be displayed on long trestles under gaily striped awnings for the canny foreigners to haggle over.

Relieved of their golden fleeces, the Cotswold Lions would trot back with their shepherds and dogs to the peace of the high pastures and wattle folds, while the wool continued its progress through the many complicated processes that would end in the production of a merchant's Sunday-best broadcloth coat, a soldier's uniform, or perhaps a billiard-cloth.

Up till the 14th century, foreign merchants, particularly from the Low Countries, were the principal buyers of Cotswold fleece, which they transported in laden carts to be processed in their own countries, but successive kings taxed the export of wool so heavily that English merchants realised it made better business sense to expand cloth-making at home, and sell finished woollen goods abroad. Records show that in the 13th century, nearly 6,000 sheep were kept at Beverston alone, while in the mid-fourteen century, during the reign of Edward III, 30,000 sacks of Gloucestershire wool were granted annually to the Court for the use of his household.

Nor was it only the English courtiers who appreciated the quality of Cotswold wool. In 1437 Don Duarte, King of Portugal, applied to King Henry VI for permission to import sixty sacksfull in order that he 'might manufacture certain cloths of gold at Florence for his own use.'

After shearing, grading and sorting the fleeces was the next step in the process of turning a sheep's coat into one suitable for a man. Those with the finest long 'staples' or strands, were set aside for combing, which produced long continuous ropes of parallel fibres known as 'tops'; while shorter wool was 'scribbled' or 'carded', whereby the strands were pulled through wooden 'hands' set with sharp hooks until the fibres were thoroughly intermingled into continuous ropes ready for spinning. During this process the various seeds and burrs which had escaped the wash would be finally dislodged.

Next the wool had to be spun and sulphur-bleached or dyed,

A competitor runs with a 60lb traditionally-shaped woolsack in the Woolsack Races at Tetbury.

using one of the many recipes for vegetable dyes handed down through the centuries. When it had been distributed among the approved spinners living in cottages lining the steep valleys, whose treadle-operated wheels whirred year-round from morning to night, the whole village seemed to be humming in unison. Spinning a good even yarn was a highly-skilled craft and very time-consuming. Everyone in the family helped: young and old, male and female. Small boys and ancient men would card 'rollags' ready for the spinsters. Most girls learnt to spin at their mother's knee, and by the age of nine or ten would have discarded the simple drop-spindle or distaff, and graduated to a fully-fledged Sleeping-Beauty type machine, whose bobbin rotated about twenty times for every turn of the spoked top-wheel.

Next it was the turn of the weavers to turn the dyed yarn into cloth. They were the aristocrats of the woollen industry, with a wealth of technical knowledge and skills passed down through generations and, formed into guilds, they proved formidable negotiators of terms and conditions with their bosses, the mill owners and cloth-merchants.

Back and forth rattled the shuttles of their sturdy hand-looms, always given pride of place in the largest room in each stone cottage, since it provided the best light and biggest work area. Like George Eliot's fictional *Silas Marner,* they were often prematurely stooped and close-sighted from long hours crouched at their looms, staring at the slowly-growing cloth for any unevenness or tangle in the yarn. Yellow-complexioned from lack of fresh air and exercise, they were nevertheless so highly regarded as reliable meal-tickets that they never lacked for village belles eager to marry them, and a good weaver could produce three yards of cloth in a day.

Fulling and scouring the cloth was a smelly business, and in the early days of the woollen trade unfortunate slaves were obliged to stand ankle-deep in tubs of human urine, trampling the cloth continuously to soften it. By medieval days the urine had been replaced by Fuller's Earth – aluminium silicate – which was easily available at Minchinhampton and did the job just as well. The slaves, in turn, were replaced by water-driven fulling mills, in which wooden hammers attached to a wheel struck the cloth at right-angles, flattening it as it rotated slowly. The fulling also mingled the fibres even more thoroughly, shrinking and – in effect – felting it until it was almost waterproof, though not surprisingly after such treatment the next important process was thorough washing.

Next it was stretched out to dry on large racks known as tenters, attached with tenterhooks to keep it taut and even out any small pockets or wrinkles that might have formed. Stealing cloth from the tenters was a hanging offence.

Another scam which was severely punished by the clothiers

was known as 'slingeing,' when oddments of cloth trimmed off the selvedge or odds and ends of woven yard would be sold directly by weavers to small workshops and there sewn into cheap garments which would find their way on to market stalls. It was difficult to prevent this practice among all the independent weavers, who could be militant if they felt their integrity was being questioned and much resented having their cottages searched.

After tenting, the dry, stretched material looked like a rather hairy felt, but by the time it had been fluffed up with teasels to raise the nap, and then carefully shorn and pressed with a hot iron, it was recognisable as top quality broadcloth, coveted all over Europe, the product upon which Gloucestershire fortunes were built as well as some of the finest houses and churches in England.

Chapter Seven

FIGHTING SPIRIT

(I)
The Sieges of Bristol and Gloucester, 1643

Ugliest of all forms of human conflict is civil war, when the fighting takes place over your own land, and you are forced to watch damage and destruction inflicted on woods and fields, roads and rivers you know like the back of your hand, seeing crops trampled, livestock slaughtered, and houses set ablaze not by hated invaders but by your very own neighbours and fellow countrymen.

A nightmare scenario, and one that engulfed England between 1642 and 1646; a bitter, cruel, lawless time when ideology was often used as cover for the settling of private quarrels. A passing army might carry off your pigs and requisition your working horses, for instance, but that didn't quite explain why your best milking cow had ended up in your neighbour's byre.

Spies and informers frequented every inn, every meeting place, and there was no one you could trust not to betray a confidence. Nor could you be sure that the Royalist general you were fighting for would not suddenly defect to Parliament, or vice versa. People swapped sides on the most trivial pretexts: it was every man for himself, and devil take the hindmost.

When the long wrangle for power between King Charles I and Parliament finally erupted into civil war in 1642, the rich cities of Gloucestershire were coveted by both sides. The Royalists, who were strongest in Wales and the West Country, were determined to control the important port of Bristol with its flourishing trade, as well as the city of Gloucester itself which, bridging the River Severn, formed an essential link for the movement of troops between England and Wales.

Pitted against the Royalist interest were the prosperous merchants of both Gloucester and Bristol, who had long suffered from the King's heavy taxes and, with a strong Puritan element within their business communities, instinctively supported the Parliamentarian cause. But when, after a long run of Royalist successes during the summer of 1642, King Charles turned his attention to Gloucestershire, he found an unexpectedly strong resistance.

From the King's base at Oxford, one army commanded by his nephew, Prince Rupert of the Rhine, advanced to join his younger brother Prince Maurice's Western royalist army at Bath, and together they marched on Bristol, where the defensive walls were being strengthened with all speed at the direction of the Governor, Colonel Nathaniel Fiennes.

He had ordered the construction of a double row of fortifications. The outer consisted of a string of forts and redoubts, connected by dry ditches and earthern ramparts. The rivers Frome and Avon together with Bristol Castle itself formed the inner defences, but since the Bristol garrison had been stripped of over a thousand men to fight in the battle of Roundway Down, which the Royalists had won, Colonel Fiennes had barely enough defenders left to man his five-mile stretch of fortifications.

After Prince Rupert had called on the city to surrender and

Originally a fortified manor house, Beverston Castle was founded by Maurice de Gaunt in 1229, and remodelled by Thomas, Lord Berkeley in the early 14th century. One side of its twin-towered gatehouse was blown up in the Civil War. Today it is a private house.

received a defiant refusal, he and his brother inspected the defences and argued over their best course of action. Cautious Maurice would have opted for a siege, but that was not the dashing Prince Rupert's style. He overruled his brother, pointing out how thinly manned the defences were, and decided that if infantry brigades attacked at four different points simultaneously, the garrison would be thrown into confusion, not knowing where best to concentrate its defence.

This, indeed, might have happened just as he predicted, had not the impetuous Cornish brigade launched their attack an hour early, at 3am instead of daybreak, forcing Rupert into action before his men were ready. Despite blocking the dry ditch in front of the city with waggons and carts, Maurice's Cornishmen found it still too deep to advance over, and all three of his attacking column commanders were killed before the scaling ladders could be hoisted into position.

Rupert's own brigades also suffered heavy casualties. His horse was killed under him, and Sir John Belasyse's infantry were repulsed.

Things looked black for the Royalists until the brigade led by Colonel Wentworth managed to evade the defenders' fire and get close enough to tear down the outer defensive wall.
Once inside it, Prince Rupert established a command post through the breached wall, while Colonel Wentworth and Sir John Belasyse's men pushed on to the inner defences, which they finally breached after two hours' fierce and bloody fighting. By now the defenders were running short of ammunition and the Governor, unwilling either to see the city destroyed or to test the loyalty of Bristol's many Royalist sympathisers, called for a parley and truce at 6pm.

Prince Rupert accepted his surrender under generous terms, allowing the defenders to march out with their arms and personal property, and though Colonel Fiennes was court-martialled for incompetence, his death sentence was later revoked.

With Bristol and its wealth in Royalist hands, now Gloucester remained the sole Parliamentarian stronghold between Wales and Lancashire. After a hasty reshuffle of his high command, the King left a detachment to garrison Bristol and himself marched with Prince Rupert and the Earl of Forth towards Gloucester.

There the young Governor, 23-year-old Colonel Edward Massie, was hard at work strengthening his defences. Gloucester's walls dated back to Roman days, but were incomplete, while its medieval castle had fallen into disrepair. Massie's urgent request to Parliament for money, supplies, and reinforcements had been ignored, so he called on the civilian population to help build earthworks. Despite his youth, Massie was a seasoned military man. He had fought in the Dutch service as a military engineer, and then on his return to England had fought in the army raised by King Charles 1 against the Scots in the so-called Bishops' War. But he was at heart a committed Presbyterian, and sided with Parliament at the outbreak of civil war in 1642, and was appointed Governor of Gloucester early in 1643.

His engineering skills came in handy in the huge task of repairing the city walls and, as the King's army approached, he ordered the suburbs to be razed to prevent the enemy using the houses as cover during an attack. He was also a man of energy and enterprise, sending out sorties to harass local Royalist strongholds, and requisitioning supplies from neighbouring farmers.

The King had no wish to suffer the heavy losses his armies had sustained at Bristol. On August 10th 1643 he sent a royal proclamation offering pardon to all in Gloucester if they would surrender at once, and when Massie boldly rejected the offer, Charles installed himself in Matson House, just outside the city, and settled down to besiege it, bombarding the walls from a distance and cutting off the water pipes so that the citizens had to drink water from the Severn and use horse mills to grind flour.

Thrown back on their own resources for food, money and war materials, the citizens proved both inventive and enterprising. Records show payments for bullets to a local pewterer and a bell founder, and cartridge paper was provided by a bookbinder named Toby Jordan. Gunpowder was made in Gloucester itself, with the vital saltpetre provided by diluted guano from Mrs Boyle's pigeon-house, while John Welstead, a local blacksmith, hammered out 64 sharpened pikes.

Massie had at his disposal two regiments of foot, plus a trained band augmented by volunteers. There were also some Scottish officers and their men, and the regiment of Colonel Nicholas Devereux, kinsman of the Earl of Essex, lord general of Parliament's army, upon whom rested Gloucester's hopes of a relieving force.

The south tower of Beverston Castle survives though twice attacked by Roundhead forces from nearby Chavenage.

The civilian population upon whom all these soldiers were billeted had to put up with much damage and deprivation, three shillings a week per man being paid to householders, and though when Sir William Waller was at Gloucester he was careful to see civilians compensated for their losses, as the siege wore on money became so scarce that only the soldiers received their pay. Officers had to do without, knowing full well that without payment their men could and would desert. Civilians who assisted the army by supplying forage or horse-power expected to be recompensed. A hastily scrawled note to the paymaster, Captain Blaney, urged him to settle an outstanding debt to *'this poor woman who brought her team to help us...what you think fit, I pray pay her, or she will scratch my eyes out.'*

Increasingly desperate pleas to London went unanswered, and with Oxford in Royalist hands, it was difficult to get messages through. Massie recruited scouts and intelligence agents under the command of Edward Donne, scoutmaster, and kept them busy. Letters would arrive from London hidden in bags of salt. Two resourceful women named Margaret Jelly and Elizabeth Beesley carried messages to Warwick, and outstanding among many feats of bravery were those of Roger Davies, who was twice captured by the Royalists and twice escaped – once with the loss of his riding-coat – and Thomas Prince of Hartpury, who 'adventured his life to go out through the king's army, creeping upon his belly, to make known the state of things in Gloucester, and brought joyful news of relief coming.'

That relief was painfully slow in arriving. The Earl of Essex had changed sides more often than most, and no one except his men really trusted him. His father had been Robert Devereux, Earl of Essex, Queen Elizabeth I's favourite, who had chanced his luck once too often and had been executed for treason in 1601. Three years later King James 1 had restored Devereux's forfeited estates to his son, whose personal life had been something of a disaster. Married as a boy to Frances Howard, daughter of the Earl of Suffolk, he had been divorced seven years later on the grounds of impotence – rather unfair since the wedding had taken place when he was only 14 – and his second venture into matrimony came to an abrupt end when his adulterous wife ran off with Sir Thomas Uvedale.

Hardly surprisingly, given this background, he was touchy, sensitive, and easily offended, quarrelling with both King James and his successor Charles 1, whose forced loans he refused adamantly to pay. Queen Henrietta Maria earned his undying hatred by having him demoted during the Bishops' War, and when the Long Parliament met in 1640, Essex emerged as the leading opposition peer in the House of Lords.

King Charles never fully trusted Essex, despite making him Lord Chamberlain. When Court gossip circulated that the King was about to arrest his principal opponents in the House of Commons, Essex warned them to go into hiding.

His high rank and long though undistinguished military experience in Germany, Spain, and the Low Countries made him the natural choice for Captain-General of the Parliamentarian forces when civil war erupted in 1642, but his preoccupation with the welfare and morale of his troops led to frequent clashes with his Parliamentary paymasters.

In June 1643, after a series of reverses, criticism of his generalship made him offer his resignation, which Parliament refused to accept, though John Pym was so worried that Essex would defect to the Royalists that he ordered an investigation into his grievances, and reluctantly agreed not only to raise reinforcements and pay his men their arrears, but also issued a public proclamation vindicating his conduct and silencing his critics.

This political wrangling was the main reason for Essex's long delay before he set out to march to the relief of Gloucester which, by late August, was in dire straits. Within the walls, hunger and sickness as well as the relentless bombardment were taking their toll on soldiers and civilians alike, while in the surrounding countryside the 25,000 troops now stationed there were stripping farms for miles around of food and forage. Once Essex was sure that he had Parliament's full backing, however, he moved fast.

Splitting the relieving force into parallel columns to take a northerly route past the Royalist stronghold at Oxford, he reunited them at Brackley in Northamptonshire, where other cavalry regiments joined them.

At Stow-on-the-Wold they were attacked by Prince Rupert with most of the King's cavalry, but after a sharp series of delaying actions Essex managed to regroup and press on towards Cheltenham. On September 5th they reached Prestbury Park – now the setting for Cheltenham racecourse – and spies brought the welcome news to the citizens of Gloucester that, rather than risk becoming trapped between Essex's force and Massie's garrison, King Charles had decided to lift the siege and retreat to Sudeley Castle.

Great was the rejoicing within the city's battered walls, and among the defenders many the sighs of relief, for in the best tradition of last-minute salvation, Massie had been down to his last three barrels of gunpowder.

FIGHTING SPIRIT

(II)
The Battle of Imjin River, 1951

The Gloucestershire Regiment – now part of the Ist battalion, The Rifles – has the distinction of carrying more battle honours on the Regimental Colours than any other British Army line regiment, but of all its military actions the Battle of the Imjin River during the Korean war still resonates most strongly with the general public.

At the end of the Second World War, the 500 mile-long Korean peninsula, which stretches south from China between the Yellow Sea and the Sea of Japan, was divided in two along the 38th Parallel, and while the Russians imposed Communism on North Korea, the South remained independent under the watchful eye of the United Nations.

When North Korea was incited by Russia to invade South Korea in June, 1950 and seize the capital, Seoul, Britain and the United States at once sent troops to support the South, and by the autumn the invaders had been forced back into their own territory. The Americans, backed by the UN, even captured North Korea's capital, Pyongyang, but in November the Chinese army intervened in strength, re-taking the city in a tit-for-tat campaign and preparing to cross the 38th Parallel again and march on Seoul.

In mid-April 1951 General Peng Duhuai, commander-in-chief of the Chinese and North Korean Forces in the field, prepared to launch his Spring Offensive with the 370,000 troops at his command. Across their line of advance, the Ist Battalion the Gloucestershire Regiment, supported by a Royal Artillery mortar battery, was thinly deployed as part of the British 29th Brigade at Solma-Ri, on the Imjin River. Since Brigadier Tom Brodie's four battalions had to cover a front of twelve miles, he deployed his men in separate positions centred upon key hills, with sizeable gaps between, and since they were not expected to hold their position long, little attempt was made to dig in or erect barbed wire defences.

The Glosters were on the left flank guarding a ford over the Imjin River which became known as Gloster Crossing. On April 22nd 1951, after their chaplain, Colonel the Reverend 'Sam' Davies, had conducted a St George's Day service a day early, reports of Chinese elements harrying their rear battalion came over the wireless, and that night General Peng's forces crossed the river in strength, and attacked the Ist Battalion the Royal Northumberland Fusiliers, driving them from their position on Hill 152, on the Glosters' right.

Heavy fighting during the night against superior numbers of enemy finally compelled the Fusiliers and also the Royal Ulster Rifles to fall back. Though they were now isolated, the Glosters continued to engage and repel the surging waves of Chinese as they tried to cross the river, but by morning they had suffered such severe casualties that in A Company only one officer remained in action.

Leaving B Company still engaged, the rest of the battalion withdrew and regrouped on Hill 235, between the Imjin river and the Seolmacheon stream – a position which became known as Gloster Hill – to make their stand, and there after facing seven separate Chinese assaults, the remaining 17 survivors in B Company joined them the following morning.

Lt Col Carne VC: a hero of the Korean War whose wooden cross, carved while in solitary confinement, now hangs in Gloucester Cathedral.

The Reverend 'Sam' Davies conducting a St George's Day service a day early at the Imjin River.

Over to the right, the battle was raging so fiercely that although three attempts were made to get tanks close enough to Hill 235 to relieve the embattled Glosters, none of them managed to make contact.

By now General Peng's attempt to seize Seoul within 36 hours of crossing the Imjin was seriously behind schedule. Wave after wave of bayonet-wielding Chinese attacked Hill 235, supported by heavy and continuous mortar and machine-gun fire, attempting to overrun the position, but despite desperate hand-to-hand fighting and severe casualties, the Glosters repulsed them again and again.

Amid the carnage, Lt Col Carne was here, there, and everywhere, encouraging his men, and he personally led two counter-attacks to drive back the enemy. Throughout he continued to send wireless messages to brigade headquarters, assuring them that all was well and his men would continue to hold on, well knowing that every hour the Chinese advance was held up gave the United Nations forces a better chance of saving Seoul.

Outstanding among the many gallant actions that day was that of 2nd lieutenant Philip Curtis, whose wife had recently died. Tasked to silence a nest of Chinese guns, he ordered his men to give him covering fire, ran forward alone and was fatally wounded. As his men raced to help him, he jumped up, snatched a grenade and with his last strength threw it into the Chinese bunker, which was destroyed.

As the dead and wounded piled up around the hill, Sam Davies the chaplain, and the medical officer, worked in the thick of the bullets, carrying in and treating the wounded and comforting the dying. Of the Glosters' 650 men when the action started, 56 had been killed and 180 wounded by April 24th, when Colonel Carne heard that the rest of the brigade was retreating to the next UN designated position, leaving the decision to him of whether to attempt to break out from the Chinese encirclement, or to surrender.

For another 24 hours of heavy fighting, the Glosters hung on to their hill against an estimated 11,000 Chinese attackers, and it was only on the morning of April 25^{th,} when 45th Field Regiment could no longer provide artillery support, that Colonel Carne organised the remains of his battalion into small, officer-led parties, and gave the order to his company commanders to make for the British lines as best they could.

Most were captured, including Colonel Carne, and, remarking, 'This looks like a holiday in Peking for some of us', the Rev Sam Davies elected to go with the wounded on the 600-mile march over six months, moving mostly by night to avoid being seen by UN aircraft, into captivity in the harsh conditions of Pi-chonig-in camp, where the prisoners stayed for the next two years. The wooden cross carved by Colonel Carne while in solitary confinement now hangs in Gloucester Cathedral.

Only the remains of D Company under the command of Major Michael Harvey managed to escape through the Chinese encirclement of Gloster Hill and several days later reached the UN lines.

Colonel Carne was awarded the Victoria Cross for his part in the battle, and posthumous awards were made of the VC to Lieutenant Philip Curtis, and the George Cross to Lieutenant Waters, who died in captivity, along with 34 other prisoners. The Rev. Sam Davies ended his ministry as the much-admired and greatly loved rector to the Gloucestershire village of Uley.

In this bloodiest of actions that began on St George's Day 1951, against overwhelming odds, the regiment heroically lived up to its nickname of The Glorious Glosters.

Chapter Eight

GREAT MEN
OF GLOUCESTERSHIRE

William Tyndale 1494–1536

The most dangerous possession a man could own in England during the early years of the sixteenth century was a copy of the Bible in his native tongue. It wasn't just a question of a fine or prison: anyone caught with an English translation of the New Testament in his house risked being arrested, tortured on the rack, whipped, immured in a dark, cold, damp prison for months, then condemned to be burnt to death at the stake.

William Tyndale, who was born at Slimbridge and brought up in south Gloucestershire, was one of the most brilliant in a generation of exceptionally learned scholars. He spoke and wrote German, French, Italian, Latin, Hebrew, Greek and Spanish as well as English. At the age of 18 he took his BA at Oxford and his MA three years later.

While studying Greek and theology at Cambridge, he became a friend of Erasmus, who had lived long enough among monks to be openly critical of their corruption, pedantry and money-grubbing ways. Some of his contempt for monastic institutions must have rubbed off on Tyndale, because when he returned to Gloucestershire to become tutor to Sir John Walsh's children at Little Sodbury, he made no bones about declaring his support for the Reformation of the Church, and often clashed with the Roman Catholic dignitaries who were entertained at Sir John's table.

It was when he acquired an illegal copy of the New Testament translated into German by Martin Luther that Tyndale was inspired with an ambition to create a similar translation in English, but in rural Gloucestershire the very idea brought him into conflict with the Church hierarchy. He was summoned to appear before the Dean of Worcester, interrogated and reprimanded, though no charges were laid against him, and the episode did nothing to restrain his determination to see the project through.

After a particularly fierce argument with a dyed-in-the-wool Catholic priest, who had claimed that people would be better off without God's laws than without the Pope's, Tyndale exclaimed, 'I defy the Pope and all his laws. If God spares my life, ere many years I will cause the boy that drives the plough to know more of scriptures than you!'

This was a highly inflammatory statement. Only ordained priests were permitted to read the Scriptures, which were written in Latin, and the suggestion that they should be made available to common people like ploughmen in their own language sent shivers down the spine of the Catholic Church. What would happen when people realised how very far from the teaching of Christ their priests had strayed? How could the Church demand payment for the forgiveness of sins, or for the shortening of time spent in Purgatory, if people were able to read for themselves that these practices were not sanctioned by Holy Writ? The Church would be threatened with the loss not only of its authority but large parts of its income as well.

When Tyndale began preaching on the same lines, the

disapproval of Church leaders in Gloucestershire became so marked that he felt obliged to move to London, hoping to find a more liberal-minded ecclesiastical hierarchy in the capital. Hoping, principally, that the Bishop of London, Cuthbert Tunstall, who had praised some of Tyndale's early writings, might back him in his great project of translating the New Testament, but in this he was disappointed. Tunstall reacted very much as the Gloucestershire clergy had done, and refused to be associated with any such translation. Brusquely he told Tyndale that he had no place for him in his household.

An alderman named Sir Humphrey Monmouth, however, welcomed him into his home, where Tyndale worked away at his translation and also preached at St Dunstan's-in-the-West. Monmouth was a cloth merchant, trading with the Continent, and may well have given his guest valuable contacts in Germany and Holland, because when it became clear to Tyndale that so great was the hostility of the Church that he would never be able to get his work published in England, he set sail for Hamburg in May, 1524.

For a time he wandered, becoming a friend of Martin Luther in Wittenberg, and often returning there to consult him even after moving to Hamburg where, working with remarkable speed, he completed his New Testament translation in 1524. The first recorded complete edition was printed and published in Worms two years later.

The next question was how to introduce it into England, where both the Church and State were implacably opposed to its distribution. Tyndale's translation was banned and burned, but nevertheless copies continued to be smuggled into the country. Some were hidden in bales of imported cloth or sacks of grain, and despite the vigilance of the authorities these were secretly passed from hand to hand like the subversive *samizdat* pamphlets of the Soviet era in Russia, though penalties for being caught with them were severe, ranging from fines and forfeiture of land to a heretic's death.

The new Archbishop of Canterbury, William Warham, arranged for his agents to buy up all the copies that were printed on the Continent, so they might be burned in bulk, but nevertheless one copy reached King Henry VIII himself, presented by Anne Boleyn, a court lady who was always abreast of the latest fashion, whether in clothes or literature. Illicit though he knew it was in the eyes of the Church, the king read Tyndale's New Testament with keen interest and approval.

Sir Thomas More, Henry's hairshirt-wearing, self-flagellating Chancellor, took a very different view. He was one of Tyndale's fiercest critics, claiming that his translation was deliberately inaccurate because he wanted to promote anti-clericalism. This was nonsense, because by working directly from Greek and Hebrew texts instead of from the Latin version of the New Testament sanctioned by the Church itself, Tyndale had in fact achieved a far more faithful translation of the original. What was more, his language was inspired: it had a lyricism, clarity and concision that have never been surpassed, and in its flexible, rhythmic beauty it is the direct precursor of Shakespeare and the great Elizabethan poets. It is generally accepted that over 80% of the Authorised Version of the Bible is in Tyndale's own words, and his phrases and images that have entered our everyday language are too numerous to count.

In comparison with Tyndale, Sir Thomas More's own writings – such as in his novel *Utopia* – appear stodgy and repetitive, and it is often difficult to disentangle his meaning from thickets of turgid prose. But instead of recognising Tyndale's great achievement, More attacked him viciously and, together with the new Bishop of London, John Stokesley, revived the penalty of burning at the stake for any heretic who possessed his work or proclaimed his views.

Undeterred, Tyndale kept on writing, printing and publishing, and the smuggling network continued to spread his criticisms, which were now aimed not only at the Catholic Church but at an even more dangerous target, Henry VIII himself. The King was desperate for a son to succeed him, but after twenty years of marriage to Katherine of Aragon, widow of his elder brother Arthur, the stunted little Princess Mary was still the only heir to the throne of England. A succession of baby boys had been stillborn or survived only a few weeks, and now Henry had begun to argue that his marriage had been accursed from the start. He should not have taken to wife his sister-in-law, since the relationship fell within the proscribed limits of the Table of Kindred and Affinity.

This was a complete reversal of his earlier argument, at the time of his wedding to Katherine, that since she and Arthur had been too young ever to consummate their marriage, she was not truly his sister-in-law and therefore it was perfectly in order for Henry, as Arthur's heir, to marry her in his place.

And why were both royal brothers so anxious to marry the same princess? Because she was the daughter of Ferdinand and Isabella, *los Reyes Catolicos* of Spain, a most important ally, and besides old Henry VII, their father, who was a miser of the first order, did not want to see Katherine's large dowry accompany her back to Spain, as it undoubtedly would if she returned there.

For Tyndale, whose uncle had been knighted during the festivities accompanying Katherine of Aragon's wedding to Prince Arthur, it was unthinkable that King Henry, to whom she had been married so long, should repudiate her in this way, particularly since the King made no secret of his desire to swap her for a younger model. He was besotted with love for the glamorous, sharp-witted, rapier-tongued Anne Boleyn, and in his pamphlet the *Practyse of Prelates* Tyndale did not mince his words when he deplored Henry's behaviour.

Hard at work as he now was on translating the Pentateuch – the first five books of the Old Testament – Tyndale really did not need another powerful enemy. He had been unable to return to England since he left London in 1523 for fear of being caught by Sir Thomas More and the Church authorities. Now, with King Henry demanding his surrender from the Holy Roman Emperor Charles V, he was truly on the run.

For five years the deadly game of cat-and-mouse continued. Spies and agents from both King and Bishop pursued the scholar from one Reformist haven to another, but even encumbered as he was with his texts and dictionaries, proofs and writing materials, Tyndale managed to evade their clutches. Friends protected him. The English merchants who lived in the Netherlands passed him from house to house, and warned him when inquisitive strangers enquired after his whereabouts.

In those years his literary output was prodigious. He worked without pause on his translations of the entire Pentateuch, plus the Books of Joshua, Judges, Ruth, Samuel, Kings and Chronicles, as well as the Book of Jonah. No one knows exactly where he was during this period of intense activity, but by 1534 the man-hunt appeared to have died down, and he emerged from hiding to lodge in the Antwerp house belonging to his friend the merchant Thomas Poyntz. It was there that, in an act of the blackest treachery, he was at last betrayed.

Handsome young Henry (Harry) Phillips's career had got off to a promising start. His father Richard was a rich man, who had stood for Parliament and twice been appointed High Sheriff of Dorset. He was also Comptroller of Customs in Poole Harbour, always a lucrative position. After Harry had obtained a degree in civil law at Oxford, he looked set to follow in his father's footsteps, but blew away his chances when he gambled and lost a large sum which Richard had entrusted to him to pay a creditor in London. Fearful of his father's wrath, Harry panicked and fled abroad.

Destitute in Antwerp three years later, he was lured back to England by the promise of a rich reward if he could discover where Tyndale was hiding and master-mind his arrest. It may have been one of the King's agents or Bishop Stokesley's who engineered this deal, but whoever was the instigator, Phillips was despatched back to the Continent in 1536, with a servant and plenty of money, with instructions to penetrate the circle of merchants who were protecting Tyndale. One by one they succumbed to young Harry's friendly charm and free-handedness with money, though Thomas Poyntz remained wary of him.

Despite his brilliant intellect, Tyndale had a simple, guileless nature. Presently he was asked to dine at a friend's house, and there met Harry Phillips, whom he found such agreeable company that he abandoned caution, reassured Poyntz of his new friend's Lutheran sympathies, and asked him back to sup at Poyntz's house.

Now Phillips had traced his quarry to his lair, he had to find a way to lure him beyond the safe haven of reformist Antwerp where he was protected by his English friends. He rode to Brussels, where the Emperor Charles held sway, collected an escort of armed men, and hurried back to Antwerp to watch Poyntz's house.

When Poyntz left home on a business trip a few days later, Phillips called at his house and, finding Tyndale alone, made an excuse to draw him out into the street. There he was seized by the armed guards, bound, and flung across a horse to be carried back to the fortress of Vilvoorde, outside Brussels. Modelled on the Bastille, in Paris, it had towers, a moat, and no fewer than three drawbridges, which made escape quite impossible.

There Tyndale was kept in terrible conditions in a dark, damp dungeon for fifteen months, pleading in vain for a candle and books so that he could continue his work. In vain, too, did Poyntz and the other English merchants in Antwerp protest against his kidnap, and even the intervention of Thomas Cromwell, who had succeeded Cardinal Wolsey as Henry VIII's right-hand man, could not persuade Archbishop Carandolet or the Governor of Vilvoorde to order his release. After a trial whose outcome was a foregone conclusion, Tyndale was tried for treason and heresy, convicted and condemned to death.

In early October 1536, he was tied to the stake amongst a heap of firewood in the town square and, just before he was strangled by the executioner and his body burned, Tyndale uttered his last prayer: 'Lord, open the King of England's eyes!'

Only three years later, his prayer was answered in a way he could hardly have dreamed. The fast-shifting sands of religious policy had changed in dramatic fashion with Henry VIII's divorce

The Tyndale Monument, near North Nibley, high above the Berkeley Vale.

from Katherine of Aragon, which caused his final break with the Pope. In 1539 he ordered that the entire Bible – in a version which drew largely on Tyndale's translations – should be published in English and that a copy should be chained to the pulpit of every church in the land.

Furthermore, a reader was appointed in each parish, so that even the illiterate should be able to hear the Bible in their native tongue, and thus make good Tyndale's claim to the Gloucestershire cleric at the very start of his career that he would 'ere many years cause the boy that drives the plough to know more of Scripture than you!'

High on the Cotswold escarpment overlooking the Bristol Channel near North Nibley stands the handsome stone tower built in 1863 to honour the Berkeley Vale's most famous son. Emerging from the narrow, rather claustrophobic spiral staircase, you are greeted with a spectacular all-round view over the Cotswolds and across the Severn to the Welsh hills. It is a fitting monument for the courageous scholar who not only brought us the Bible in English and paid for it with his life, but also left us with language of a power and beauty that no author who followed him has been able to surpass.

Edward Jenner 1749–1823

Looking for a true English hero to fill the vacant plinth in Trafalgar Square? Someone who saved lives without number, and helped to rid the world of the scourge of a killer disease? Surely it is high time to bring back the fine statue of Edward Jenner by William Calder Marshall, which was installed there in 1858 with the enthusiastic support of Prince Albert, but after the death of Victoria's consort was quietly removed to a less glorious site among the fountains and pools of Kensington Garden.

Why? Could it have been because people thought a country doctor looked out of place among the dashing military and naval heroes? But Edward Jenner was rather more than a country doctor, and though poorly rewarded by his own compatriots, even in his own lifetime his fame had spread throughout the world.

A Gloucestershire man through and through, he was born and bred, worked and died in the Berkeley Vale on the banks of the River Severn. Edward was the second youngest of the Rector of Berkeley's nine children. When he was five, both his parents died, and he was brought up thereafter by his older sister Mary, who married the Rev. G.C. Black, Berkeley's new incumbent.

After attending school first at Wotton-under-Edge and then Cirencester, when he was thirteen he was apprenticed for seven years to Daniel Ludlow, a local surgeon. Never happier than when roaming the countryside, young Edward used every opportunity to escape from his medical duties to pursue his passion for natural history, collecting birds' eggs, fossils, and other interesting objects along the banks of the Severn, whose low-lying, marshy fringes make the Berkeley Vale a paradise for waterfowl. The surrounding wooded hills were also full of the wildlife that proved of absorbing interest to the young naturalist.

He moved to London at the age of 21 to continue his studies with John Hunter, then on the staff of St George's Hospital, who was not only an eminent surgeon and the foremost medical tutor in Britain, but also highly respected as a biologist and experimental scientist. Open-minded and forward-thinking himself, he always urged his pupils to observe and experiment – advice which in young Edward Jenner's case fell on fertile ground. In the next years his insatiable curiosity, independence of thought and willingness to challenge accepted wisdom made him both friends and detractors in the medical establishment.

He and John Hunter hit it off at once and maintained a lively correspondence for the rest of Hunter's life. He gave Jenner one of his own precious thermometers to measure the temperature of hibernating mammals as well as for use on human patients and, when he broke it, good-naturedly sent him another – together with a few well-chosen remarks about his clumsiness.

One of Jenner's first letters to his mentor records his observation of cuckoos, and explains how a cuckoo chick will push its foster parents' own chicks out of the nest in order to benefit from sole occupation and the food brought by both birds. This view contrasted sharply with that of Aristotle, who thought that it was the foster-mother who pushed her own chicks out of the nest; or later naturalists who claimed that the mother cuckoo was the culprit, or that the true-born nestlings died of starvation because the cuckoo chick ate all the food.

Much later, in a paper which earned him election to the Royal Society, Jenner explained that the newly-hatched cuckoo chick has a special depression in its back between the wings, enabling it to cup an egg or nestling in it and then retreat backwards to the rim of the nest, before pushing the rival over and out, and this action the cuckoo repeats until it is the nest's sole occupant. By the twelfth week of its life, however, the cuplike depression has disappeared.

The reason for this strange behaviour, Jenner argued, is that the hen cuckoo, arriving in England in mid-April and leaving for the south in mid-July, does not have time to build a nest, lay and incubate her own eggs, and rear the chicks herself until they are strong enough flyers to migrate themselves – a process that takes 15 weeks. Hence her reliance on the charity of other birds to rear her young.

Though many of his critics dismissed his paper on cuckoos as absurd, with the invention of photography Jenner's view was shown to be entirely accurate, and in a way this small episode characterised his approach to any branch of science, bringing a fresh mind free of preconceived ideas to each problem, then backing careful observation and assessment of indicators with a dogged determination to find out its cause and, in medical matters, its cure.

In the case of smallpox, there were plenty of preconceived ideas and theories for the treatment of this long-dreaded scourge which, from time out of mind, had been one of mankind's biggest killers. The horrible sight of people dying slowly from the disease, which ate away their skin until finally the pain killed them, was hauntingly familiar in every human settlement. It is thought to have originated in Northern Africa and been spread eastward by traders from ancient Egypt. Early Chinese and Indian Sanskrit texts refer to its ravages. There is evidence of smallpox-type skin lesions on the faces of Egyptian mummies as far back as the 18th Dynasty (1570 BC) and Ramses V who died in 1156 BC is similarly scarred.

Spreading west again by slow degrees along the Silk Road, smallpox eventually reached Europe, and the severe epidemic of 108 AD coincided with the early stages of the Roman Empire's decline. Throughout the medieval period, the disease was a recurrent menace in one country after another, and successive waves of expansion and conquest by Arabs and Crusaders alike contributed to its spread.

It caused particular havoc in the New World, for when Spanish and Portuguese *conquistadores* penetrated the forests and mountain fastnesses of South America, they brought with them a virus against which the native tribes had no immunity. Incas, Mayans and Aztecs died in thousands, and the same thing happened to the Native Americans at the coming of the early settlers.

Characterised by a high fever, itching red pustules, risk of blindness and subsequent scarring in those who survived, smallpox was reckoned to kill 400,000 people annually in Europe alone, and during the early nineteenth century the 'speckled monster,' as it was known, proved fatal to 98% of the babies who contracted it.

Yet from as far back as the third century BC it was known that anyone who survived an attack would thereafter be immune to the disease and could nurse the sick with impunity. The many often-painful and perfectly ineffective methods of treatment ranged from keeping the patient half-naked in a constant draught and administering twelve bottles of small beer every 24 hours, to branding with a hot iron, but the only procedure with any appreciable success was the Asiatic system of 'variolation' which Lady Mary Wortley Montague encountered in Turkey in 1717 while her ambassador husband was en poste at the court of the Ottoman Emperor.

In her own words: *The small-pox, so fatal, and so general among us, is here entirely harmless, by the invention of engrafting, which is the term they give it. There is a set of old women, who make it their business to perform the operation, every autumn, in the month of September, when the great heat is abated.*

People send to one another to know if any of their family has a mind to have the small-pox; they make parties for this purpose, and when they are met... the old woman comes with a nut-shell full of the matter of the best sort of small-pox, and asks what vein you please to have opened. She immediately rips open that you offer to her, with a large needle (which gives you no more pain than a common scratch) and puts into the vein as much matter as can lie upon the head of her needle...

The children or young patients play together for the rest of the day, and are in perfect health to the eighth (day). *Then the fever begins to seize them, and they keep their beds two days, very seldom three. They have very rarely above twenty or thirty* (pocks) *in their faces, which never mark, and in eight days' time they are as well as before their illness...*

Every year thousands undergo this operation, and the French Ambassador says pleasantly that they take the small-pox here by way of diversion, as they take the waters in other countries...

Lady Mary herself had had painful experience of smallpox, which had marked her face badly and killed her 20 year old brother, and so impressed was she by the success of this Turkish treatment that she not only had her own son and daughter 'engrafted' in the same way, but on her return to England spread the word among her wide circle of friends. Since these included many of the aristocracy and members of the Royal family, the procedure rapidly became fashionable.

As an initial precaution, the royal pardon was extended to six convicts who agreed to act as guinea-pigs for Dr Charles Maitland, and when all of them – as well as a test panel of orphaned children – survived the treatment, now referred to as 'variolation,' the Princess of Wales gave permission for Dr Maitland to repeat it on her own daughters, and soon most of London society had followed suit.

It became apparent, however, that Lady Mary's blithe declaration that in Turkey smallpox was 'entirely harmless,' was a considerable overstatement, for 2 or 3% of variolated patients did develop full-blown smallpox after the process. Some died, some were scarred for life, and some developed tuberculosis or syphilis. Nevertheless the treatment continued to increase in popularity

Detail of a pastel portrait by W.R.Le Fanu of Dr Edward Jenner, 'Vaccine Clerk to the World,' which was exhibited at the Royal Academy in 1800.

throughout the first half of the eighteenth century, particularly among European royalty who had suffered heavy losses in the early 1700s.

The Empress Maria Theresa of Austria had her large family variolated, young and old, and so did Catherine the Great of Russia. Frederick the Great of Prussia went one better and insisted that his entire army underwent the treatment.

Similarly, in America, an epidemic in Boston in 1721 resulted in 6,000 out of a population of 12,000 contracting the disease, but only 2% of the variolated patients died, a startling improvement on the usual 14%, and this persuaded many Americans to seek protection against smallpox in this way over the ensuing decades.

Twenty years later in rural Gloucestershire, Dr Edward Jenner had begun to focus his attention on smallpox – some of his attention, that is, because he was simultaneously making observations and experiments in many unrelated fields. He had a rather scattergun approach to science: so many subjects interested him in that exciting age of discovery that he tended to flit from one to another without subjecting each to the analytic rigour demanded today.

Zoology and natural history had always been close to his heart, and during his two years' study under John Hunter's tutelage, he had helped to arrange the many zoological specimens accumulated by the naturalist Joseph Banks during Captain James Cook's first voyage of discovery in the Pacific. When offered the chance to act as official naturalist on Cook's second voyage, however, he declined, preferring to practise medicine and pursue his many other interests back at home in the Severn Vale.

Indeed, he had plenty to occupy him in Gloucestershire. Besides writing his paper on the nesting habits of the cuckoo, he studied geology, and also successfully built his own hydrogen balloon on the Montgolfier model which, on September 2nd 1784, flew from the courtyard of Berkeley Castle to Kingscote on the escarpment, badly scaring a party of harvesting reapers. He galloped ten miles to catch up with it, paid his respects to Catherine Kingscote, the young lady he was to marry four years later, and relaunched the balloon, which drifted onwards to Birdlip Hill near Cheltenham, some 24 miles in all, touching down near a pub known thereafter as the *Air Balloon*.

He carried out experiments on human blood, but was disappointed to find that it did not materially improve his raspberry crop. He was also very interested in the strategies birds and mammals adopted in order to survive in winter. Using John Hunter's thermometer, he assiduously measured the temperature of hibernating hedgehogs, and began to question the accepted view that swallows buried themselves in river mud when they disappeared in late summer.

They were, he pointed out, neither hungry nor dirty when they returned in the spring, and the specimens he dissected had full crops. Sailors had reported seeing swallows far out to sea, and he speculated that despite the enormous distances, the birds might overwinter in Africa.

He played the violin in a musical group, wrote poetry and light verse, and maintained a wide-ranging learned correspondence with many scientific luminaries including Erasmus Darwin, grandfather of the author of *The Origin of Species;* Sir Humphry Davy, and his old friend John Hunter.

A man of many interests, with a friendly, engaging manner, he could be the life and soul of a party so long as he was among friends, though to the London medical fraternity who mocked his experiments and accused him of a lack of scientific rigour he showed a frostier side. It was more important to him to be liked and trusted by his patients, even when he chose to use them as guinea-pigs for his experiments. He was as energetic physically as he was mentally, riding great distances to visit patients up and down the vale from Bristol in the south to Gloucester in the north, an area of 400-odd square miles. He also ran a thriving practice in Cheltenham and another in London, but it was his work in connection with smallpox that brought him to worldwide attention.

The Berkeley Vale with its lush pastures is classic dairying country and, like everyone closely associated with those who work on the land, Jenner knew that even in the wildest of the 'old wives' tales' that get passed down from one generation to the next, there is generally a kernel of truth. In Gloucestershire, in particular, country lore had long maintained that dairymaids had special protection against smallpox.

'I shall never get those ugly marks on my face, for I have had the cowpox,' Jenner had heard a dairymaid declare in his youth, and the remark had stuck in his mind. Cowpox was a common viral disease of cattle which caused scabby lesions on teats and udder, and was readily transmissible to the women who milked them; but, crucially, both in humans and cattle the infection was relatively mild and the fever only lasted a few days. Could the lesser disease, he wondered, really protect against the greater?

The only way to find out was by experiment. In May 1796 Jenner, by then in his forties and well-respected locally, took pus from the lesions on the hands of Sarah Nelmes, a young dairymaid who had caught cowpox from one of her milkers named Blossom, and introduced it into a scratch on the arm of James Phipps, the eight-year-old son of his gardener. A few days later James ran a temperature and went off his food, but by the tenth day he had recovered.

After giving him six weeks to recuperate fully, Jenner embarked on the second, and far more dangerous, part of his experiment, this time inoculating James with real smallpox pus. After what must have been an anxious wait both for Dr Jenner and the boy's parents, during which young James showed no symptoms and continued in robust health, Jenner became convinced that the cowpox treatment had worked, rendering James wholly immune to smallpox.

He named the procedure 'vaccination' since the active agent was derived from *vacca* – a cow – and it was a bitter disappointment to him when his paper describing the successful experiment on James Phipps was rejected by the Royal Society. He persevered with other patients, however, and the following year published a pamphlet entitled: *An Inquiry into the Causes and Effects of the Variolae Vaccinae, a disease discovered in some of the western counties of England, particularly Gloucestershire and known by the name of Cow-Pox,* but despite all his efforts to publicise the success of his treatment, the medical establishment continued to shun him and refused to accept his claims.

Nor were there any takers when he travelled to London to seek volunteers for vaccination, though a few medical colleagues to whom he had given the cowpox inoculant began to circulate the treatment among their own patients.

Closing ranks in order to protect the healthy incomes they were deriving from the now-accepted practice of variolation, the British medical establishment scorned Jenner's claim that his

Hair and horns from Blossom, the cow from which Sarah Nelmes caught cowpox. The horns are one of several pairs reputed to be from Blossom. Her hide is still preserved in St. George's Hospital, London.

Horns of Blossom, the cow which gave Sarah Nelmes the milkmaid cowpox, from which unlovely source Jenner cleverly developed his vaccination technique which proved so much safer than variolation against smallpox.

The Temple of Vaccinia, in the garden of Jenner's home, The Chantry, Berkeley — now the Edward Jenner Museum.

own treatment was far safer. They also resented having to rely on him for supplies of cowpox pus, not readily available in London, while some opposed vaccination on the ridiculous grounds that, because the agent was derived from beasts of the field — God's lower creatures, as they put it — they feared they might grow cloven hoofs or sprout horns, an absurdity illustrated in James Gillray's well-known cartoon which shows cows erupting from patients' arms and faces as the vaccine is introduced.

Undeterred, Jenner soldiered on with his experiments, and soon perfected a method of extracting pus from human cowpox lesions and drying it on to lengths of thread, so that it could easily be transported. He reported every development in his research to his wide circle of correspondents, both in England and abroad and slowly, over the next decade, his method of vaccination gained acceptance in Europe and America until it entirely supplanted variolation.

In contrast to the indifference of the British medical establishment, other countries were quick to take advantage of Dr Jenner's Marvellous Medicine. Even though Britain and France were at war, Napoleon Bonaparte seized on the opportunity to protect his soldiers, and had his whole army vaccinated, while singing Jenner's praises in extravagant terms.

'Ah, Jenner, I can deny that man nothing!' he exclaimed when the doctor wrote to ask for the release of medical colleagues interned during the war, and let them go at once.

'Vaccine Clerk to the World,' Jenner styled himself, only

Eccentric woodwork decorates the entrance door of the Temple of Vaccinia in the Jenner Museum at Berkeley.

partly in jest, because he spent so much of his time supplying and writing about cowpox that he had barely enough left to run his own medical practices. He was curiously indifferent to commercial opportunities and never tried to capitalise on his discovery. Poor people who could not afford to pay for vaccination would assemble for free treatment at 'The Temple of Vaccinia,' as he named the little thatched hut in his garden which a friendly clergymen had built for him.

He was far more interested in exploring the frontiers of science than in making money, and never tried to charge his fellow doctors for using the treatment he had pioneered. Nevertheless, in recognition of his work and the losses he had suffered in pursuing it, his friends persuaded the British Government to make him an award of £10,000 in 1802, and followed up this bounty with £20,000 in 1807.

Further honours began to accrue: honorary degrees and membership of universities around the world. He was awarded the freedom of London, Edinburgh, Glasgow and Dublin. The Empress of Russia gave him a ring, and Napoleon had a special medal minted to recognise his achievements, but fame in one field never blunted Jenner's curiosity and desire to explore others.

A particularly long-lasting enthusiasm had been sparked by the fossils he collected as a boy, and in later life, as a member of the Geological Society, his most spectacular find was the fossilised remains of a sea monster which he named a Plesiosaur – a kind of huge prehistoric lizard – at the base of nearby Stinchcombe Hill. He had long believed that fossils were monuments to a departed world rather than relics of currently extant animals, and here was the proof.

He and his wife Catherine, formerly Miss Kingscote, lived in The Chantry, a handsome house in Berkeley which is now the Edward Jenner Museum, full of fascinating pictures, papers and mementoes of his diverse interests, including a selection of horns

William Calder Marshall's statue of Edward Jenner, originally placed in Trafalgar Square, was removed to Kensington Gardens in London after the death of his supporter Prince Albert.

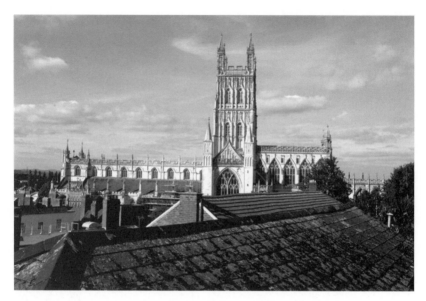

Gloucester Cathedral accepted the first memorial statue to the pioneer of vaccination, Dr Edward Jenner.

alleged to have belonged to Sarah Helms the milkmaid's famous cow, Blossom, which had proliferated in the way the relics of saints are apt to. Unfortunately his wife was delicate, and her health a perennial worry. Of his four children, his oldest son, Edward, had inherited his mother's frail constitution and died of tuberculosis at the age of 21, while Catherine herself succumbed to the same disease in 1815.

For the last eight years of his life, Jenner remained as busy as ever, but the hostility of London's medical establishment against the maverick country doctor increased rather than diminished as vaccination gradually replaced variolation (which was eventually banned). Even those who, like the fashionable doctor George Mosley, used Jenner's method, never acknowledged his achievement, and when he died of a stroke in January, 1823, his funeral was a local affair which none of his London colleagues attended.

Appropriately, Gloucester Cathedral was first to accept a marble memorial statue of Jenner, wearing a doctor's formal robes, commissioned by his friend John Baron and the Provincial Grand Lodge of Freemasons, of which Jenner had been a member. After scrutinising it carefully, the forthright parson Francis Witts remarked to his diary: *It cannot be called a correct resemblance of Jenner; but at any period of his life he was a very unsuitable study for a sculptor, the figure broad, thickset, clumsy and the countenance coarse, though very intelligent when lighted up by the talent within.* Handsome is as handsome does, however, and other countries were generous in their own tributes to his outstanding contribution to the fight against smallpox.

Nevertheless, the faint disapproval of the English medical establishment towards the forthright country doctor, together with an unspoken resentment of his achievements lingered on, and it was well over thirty years before a committee of London doctors raised enough money by subscription to erect William Calder Marshall's statue in Trafalgar Square. Even for this the principal donations came from America and Russia.

Four years later, the seated statue with only the tiny head of a cow on the crossbar of the chair to hint at the nature of Jenner's achievement, was moved to its present site in Kensington Gardens, proof indeed that a prophet is not without honour except in his own country.

Perhaps the satirical magazine *Punch* put it best when it wrote:

England's ingratitude still blots
The escutcheon of the brave and free
I saved you many million spots,
And now you grudge one spot for me

Bring back Jenner to Trafalgar Square!

Peter Scott, Conservationist 1909–1989

The world-famous Wildfowl and Wetland Trust at Slimbridge, on the marshy margin of the River Severn, could be said to owe its existence to the last letter written to his wife by Captain Robert Falcon Scott, as he set out for the Antarctic expedition in which he would perish. *'Make the boy interested in natural history, if you can,'* he advised her. *'It is better than games.'*

Seldom can parental advice have had more beneficial effects on wildlife conservation in general throughout the world, and the wildfowl of Gloucestershire in particular.

'The boy' was Captain Scott's two-year-old son and only child Peter, born of his brief marriage to the sculptor and society beauty Kathleen Bruce. A woman of great charm and high spirits, she took an unconventional approach to child-rearing, encouraging Peter to spend his early years barefoot in all weathers, winter and summer, wearing only a kind of specially-designed belted tunic and coming indoors as little as possible. This regime, she believed, would ward off childhood illness, and certainly it made the boy extremely hardy and largely impervious to discomfort, heat or cold, which was to stand him in good stead in later life.

She also encouraged his interest in music and drawing, and fostered his passion for wildlife which frequently left her in charge of an eclectic mix of lizards, snakes, owls and injured small birds in their London house. She would be bombarded with letters advising her how to care for them while Peter was at school. Kathleen was clever and very attractive, with a wide acquaintance among the great and good of Edwardian society. Prime Ministers and musicians, actors and Fellows of the Royal Society sat for their portraits while Peter lay on the studio floor, busy with his own drawings, and frequent converse with his mother's distinguished visitors gave him a friendly ease of manner that opened many doors and contributed much to his success.

Both at West Downs preparatory school and later at Oundle, he preferred pursuing and observing wildlife to work in the classroom, and did just the minimum required by his teachers. Not that he always escaped retribution. 'I think I was beaten more often than any other fellow in my year,' he remarked stoically, but the experience never appeared to bother him, despite his mother's indignation. It wasn't that he was particularly lazy, simply indifferent to lessons that did not relate to his private interests.

Fur, feather, scale or fin, wildlife of every kind fascinated him, but birds he loved best of all. At Oundle, owls would pop up from within his desk, and lizards and geckos lurked in his wardrobe. When he went to Trinity College, Cambridge, to read Natural Sciences, he netted in most of his bedroom to create an aviary, somewhat to the inconvenience of the friend who shared

Swans by the Visitor Centre at Slimbridge Wildfowl and Wetland reserve at the Dumbles between the Sharpness canal and the river Severn.

the rooms. But Natural Sciences, with their heavy emphasis on the bones of dead animals rather than living ones, did not hold his attention long, and with his mother's approval he switched to History of Art. The first money he earned was from drawing portraits of his friends and contemporaries.

He had inherited his mother's artistic skill, and was fortunate in having her enthusiastic backing as well as her wide acquaintance and large family whom she dragooned into attending Peter's first exhibition of paintings in London in 1933. Kathleen herself had been the youngest of eleven children, so her son had plenty of cousins, uncles and aunts, and word soon spread throughout London society of his exceptional talent for painting wildlife, particularly birds. Though he began with water-colours, he soon switched to oils, in which medium he worked quickly and with great facility, often on several paintings simultaneously. His technique was to sketch in the sky, vegetation and water first, and then add birds as the focal point, taking great pains in capturing their plumage, movement, and attitude. His first paintings sold readily, and whatever he produced continued to do so all his life.

Meantime he was exploring other interests, most of them connected with water and the sea. Sailing was a particular passion. In 1936 he represented his country in the Olympic Games, and won a Bronze Medal. He had a highly competitive nature and once something gripped his enthusiasm he could not rest until he excelled in it. He loved skating, and also became an enthusiastic glider pilot, but none of these activities were so close to his heart as painting, observing, classifying and, of course, shooting wildfowl.

Like most well-known conservationists, in his youth he was a very keen hunter of the species he would spend most of his later life fighting to preserve. He was a good shot, and spent much of his late teens and early twenties flighting wildfowl on the saltings by the Wash. In a flat-bottomed boat equipped with a muzzle-loading punt-gun, he and a companion would glide through the rushes in pursuit of ducks and geese in the freezing winter dawn, immobile and wet through, and in mortal peril of being stunned by the recoil of the antiquated weapon.

After his mother's remarriage to Lord Kennet, a distinguished politician who was also an enthusiastic ornithologist, and buoyed up by two sell-out one-man exhibitions of his paintings, Peter bought a lighthouse on the Wash near Sutton Bridge. Here, after careful study of traditional methods of decoying ducks and geese into nets, he started to build up a collection of his own wildfowl. Some he bought from dealers, some had been netted and others were survivors that had been shot but merely wing-tipped.

Two books about birds were published by *Country Life,* and he worked spasmodically on painting commissions, though never very hard. The chance to go shooting in Northern Ireland or Hungary or Iran, or to research some new aspect of bird habitat or behaviour, always took priority over work. To his mother's despair, he had a cavalier attitude to money, spent far more than he earned, and had to be chased into completing commissions in time. Once she had to work shoulder-to-shoulder with him to complete a big canvas for an American buyer, and the paint was barely dry when he collected it on his way home.

In 1939 at the outbreak of the Second World War, Peter joined the Royal Naval Volunteer Reserve, known as the Wavy Navy because of the serpentine gold bands on their sleeves, as a Probationary Temporary Sub-Lieutenant, from which lowly rank he rose meteorically to achieving his own command after barely three years. After an uncomfortable spell in a destroyer, HMS *Broke,* guarding convoys in the North Atlantic, he won the DSC (Distinguished Service Cross) and Bar while commanding a squadron of gun boats guarding the English Channel against German E-boats. He made use of his old skills in camouflaging bird-watching hides to disguise the superstructure of ships under his command, and launched more than one raid on the French coast to pick up stranded British servicemen.

In March, 1944, he took up the job of right-hand man to his friend Christopher Dreyer, senior staff officer to the Captain of Coastal Forces in the Channel, who was in charge of deploying all the craft in the protective screen around the D-Day fleet when they launched their invasion of Normandy.

Deep in the network of underground galleries and tunnels beneath Dover Castle, which had been enlarged and converted from their use as a military hospital to a coastal command centre, was The Plot: a 25ft table covered in a map on which were placed models of every ship afloat in the area, their movements plotted by radar stations on Beachy Head, Ventnor and Portland Bill. There the planners lived like troglodytes, working long hours and at close quarters. Cooks, clerks, generals, admirals, administrators and politicians came and went in this crowded rabbit-warren which was, in Peter's words, 'Pretty fair bedlam,' but astonishingly its security was never compromised, and complete tactical surprise was achieved when Operation Overlord swung into action on the morning of June 6, 1944.

By the time Peter left the Navy in 1945 at the end of the war, his short-lived marriage to the aspiring young writer Elizabeth Jane Howard was also nearly over. Despite efforts on both sides to patch it up during a visit to America, (from which they returned on the *Queen Mary* accompanied by boxes containing snakes, frogs, terrapins, tortoises and alligators, all labelled *Fragile. Cabin Only*) in 1947 she left him and their daughter Nicola, and went to search for a publisher for her novel.

One of Peter's rare failures was to capture the Parliamentary seat of Wembley North for the Conservatives in the Labour landslide victory of 1945, but from the point of view of wildlife, this was a blessing in disguise. During the war, his wildfowl collection at the East Lighthouse had been dispersed and the building itself was no longer on the water's edge, for the land had been drained and the sea driven back.

Searching for a new home for his birds, he accepted an invitation to see the huge flocks of migratory geese that came from Russia to overwinter on the saltings of the River Severn. Peter was particularly interested in the Lesser Whitefronted goose (*Anser erythropus*), which he believed was not such a rare visitor to Britain as ornithologists then believed. To his delight on that first visit he saw several Lesser Whitefronts among the large flocks of Common Whitefronts, and decided there and then to establish a conservation and scientific study centre for the world's wildfowl on the banks of the Severn near the village of Slimbridge. It was – as he described it – 'a moment of unforgettable exultation... an epoch-making occurrence, a turning point.'

He flung himself heart and soul into this new venture. In the spring of 1946, Captain Robert Berkeley of Berkeley Castle was persuaded to lease him 23 acres of The Dumbles, as the land between the river and the Sharpness canal was called, with the proviso that the landlord retained the right to shoot geese there several times a year, and a small, devoted team augmented by German prisoners-of-war awaiting repatriation set to work to fence in the marshy ground, dig ponds and construct pens, as well as planting trees and shrubs, with paths round which barrowloads of feed could be taken to the captive birds.

As usual, the biggest problem was finance. Peter was open-handed with money – on one occasion emptying his wallet to fund a hitch-hiker's voyage to Australia – and spent much faster than he earned. Although his pictures sold handsomely, he was always trying to catch up with his artistic commitments, and could pay his staff only a pittance for all their hard work.

Nevertheless the collection grew rapidly, most birds were acquired by legal means (though once an over-trusting pair of

Tufted ducks in St James's Park were unceremoniously grabbed and relocated), and in the autumn of 1946 the Severn Wildfowl Trust was formally established to share the financial burden.

Splitting his time between painting in his London studio, collecting birds and soliciting grants and donations for the development of the wildfowl trust, Peter was in perpetual motion. He had now discovered a talent for broadcasting which was eagerly seized upon by the BBC, and gave fund-raising lectures which raised his public profile. It was a heavy blow when his mother, who had given unstinting support to all his projects, died of cancer in 1947, but he still had the energy for yet another venture, launching the Inland Waterways Association to preserve Britain's historic canals, just a few months before the wildfowl trust came into being.

Despite putting so much effort and skill into preserving his birds, he was still a keen shot, and it was not until the early 1950s that he put aside his guns. According to his autobiography, it was the sight of a wounded goose's long-drawn-out suffering over two days on mud-flats where neither dog nor man could retrieve it, that finally turned him against shooting, and thereafter he took no pleasure in it, preferring, as he said, to catch live geese instead of distributing mouldering corpses.

Another kind of shooting, however, he took to with enthusiasm. This was for rocket-launched nets to capture wild geese, which were then ringed and released in order to study migration patterns across the world. From North to South America, to the Arctic and Australia, he ranged ever more widely, observing, collecting, lecturing and, when Bristol acquired a television studio, becoming a regular interviewer and presenter of *Look*, a Nature programme which rapidly acquired an audience of millions.

His marriage in 1951 to the talented photographer Philippa Talbot-Ponsonby, in a ceremony performed by the Minister of the British Legation in Reykjavik, cemented a working partnership that had already endured since the foundation of the wildfowl trust at Slimbridge.

Once he had sold his guns, all his energy was directed to preserving endangered species and, equally important, their natural habitat. Not only of birds, either. 'His enthusiasm for everything to do with conservation or the animal world would warm you like a fire,' commented the naturalist and author Gerald Durrell. 'Half an hour's talk with Peter and you felt you could succeed in realising your wildest dreams.'

When the World Wildlife Fund was founded in 1961, he played a leading role in persuading Prince Bernhard of the Netherlands to accept the international presidency, with Prince Philip, Duke of Edinburgh, as President of the British national appeal. He also designed the universally engaging logo of the panda, and made a significant contribution to the Survival Service Commission by creating the loose-leaf Red Data books listing critically-endangered species and habitats.

Slowly, over the next forty years, public awareness grew of the damage humans were doing to the environment and the animals with which they share it, and whenever a campaign was launched, whether to save whales, tigers, the polar regions or the Galapagos, Peter became involved.. His wide acquaintance and outstanding powers of persuasion made him indispensable to the continual battle to raise funds and change the behaviour of governments, but money was always a major problem. If there was a choice of spending scarce resources on humans or saving animals threatened with extinction, the animals always lost out.

'Keep your pecker up!' he told a colleague who was feeling the strain of operating on a shoestring. 'We shan't save all, but we'll save a jolly lot more than if we'd never existed.'

It was with the same robust good sense tinged with idealism that he rested his case for conservation on what he called his 'four pillars'. First, in an ethical sense, Man has no more right to the planet than the other creatures who share it. Second came the aesthetic case: since the works of nature are just as beautiful as the works of Man, it is equally wrong to destroy either. Third, in a scientific sense, it is an act of vandalism to destroy any creature or

The bust of Sir Peter Scott, 'patron saint of conservation,' at Slimbridge.

plant whose use to mankind is still unknown; and fourth, there is the economic case, which points out that poor countries which preserve their wildlife benefit from money rich tourists bring from their own wildlife-depleted countries.

Painfully slowly at first, and then with increasing attention, the British public began to listen, and Peter's role in changing attitudes to wildlife was recognised in 1973 when he received the first-ever knighthood for Services to Conservation.

The rest of the world was a different matter. After countless visits to the Middle East, pulling every string he could command, he still failed to persuade the rulers of Iran, Oman, and Arabia of the importance of his mission and the urgent need for funds. Iceland, too, disappointed him by its refusal to sign the moratorium on whaling; in disgust he returned his Icelandic Order of the Falcon.

Meanwhile, despite its founder's distraction with worldwide conservation projects, the Wildfowl and Wetlands Trust at Slimbridge had flourished and expanded out of all recognition. The crumbling cottage and farm buildings had grown into a large, modern visitor centre, complete with lecture halls, research laboratories, and an immense car park filled with tourist coaches as well as private cars; and the well-maintained network of ponds and pens, hides and flowering shrubs now covered much more than the original 23 acres.

Subsidiary wildfowl reserves at Martin Mere on the west coast of Lancashire, Peakirk in Cambridgeshire, and Welney in the Fens, were reinforced by another five scattered around the country, each with its own distinctive character but all providing migratory birds with safe overwintering conditions, and the public with a chance to see them from the warmth and comfort of well-equipped observatories. Slimbridge remained the hub, though, and as visitors watched the magical display of uncountable geese, ducks and swans swooping from the sky to land on

Swan Lake as dusk fell they were often unaware that only a few yards away in his own house overlooking the lake, Peter was at his easel, painting the same nightly spectacle.

It was there in Gloucestershire that he died shortly before his eightieth birthday, leaving unfinished his design for his latest venture: a wildfowl reserve at Barnes in the London borough of Richmond-on-Thames, which was eventually opened in 2000 and is known as the London Wetland Centre.

Sir David Attenborough called Peter Scott the 'patron saint of conservation', because although he was by no means the first to realise the damage that human exploitation is causing to the world's wildlife and the environment, his commitment, vision and energy, as well as his skill in communicating through mass media, conveyed the urgency of the problem to a wider public than ever before. He was a mover and shaker, who changed the mindset of people and governments in a way earlier conservationists could only dream of, warning the world that the earth, the sea, the sky and all the species they support are in danger of being destroyed by human activity.

Has the message reached us soon enough to reverse the destruction? That is a question that only time can answer.

Ralph Vaughan Williams 1872–1958

The peaceful Gloucestershire village of Down Ampney, a few miles outside Cirencester, mentioned in the Domesday Book and little changed since then, seems a thoroughly appropriate birthplace for this composer, whose music is so powerfully evocative of the English countryside. Indeed, despite his Welsh name, Ralph Vaughan Williams can be said to be the first to give English music a true national voice distinct from the fashionable – largely Germanic – influences of the nineteenth century.

But although much later he honoured Down Ampney by naming one of his most celebrated hymn tunes – *Come down, O love divine* – after his birthplace, he didn't actually live there for long. His father died when RVW was two, and his mother took him with her other two children to live at Leigh Hill Place, her family home in Surrey. She was a Wedgwood, a member of the prominent and prosperous family descended from Josiah Wedgwood, founder of the famous pottery firm, inter-related by marriage several times over with those of Erasmus Darwin, and the combined families had produced intellectual pioneers in many different fields, including at least ten Fellows of the Royal Society.

Ralph's first piano lessons were given by his aunt Sophy Wedgwood, but he found the instrument a struggle and was better suited by the violin, which he described as 'my salvation'. Nor did he shine musically at Charterhouse, and although he took organ lessons with Charles Wood at Cambridge, his tutor regarded him as 'hopelessly unhandy', and advised him not to consider a career as an organist.

Before that, however, a spell at the Royal College of Music under the guidance of Hubert Parry, a fellow Gloucestershire man, greatly improved his understanding of harmony, and when he returned there at the end of his years at Cambridge he made a friend who would have a lifelong effect on his music, Gustav Holst. Though their styles could hardly have been more different – Vaughan Williams still ploddingly undeveloped at that stage and Holst mercurially brilliant – each understood the other's strengths and weaknesses, and together they enjoyed what they called 'field days', good-humouredly deconstructing and analysing one another's work to mutual benefit.

Vaughan Williams had been lucky to be born with – as he himself put it – a 'very small silver spoon in my mouth', and this private income enabled him to continue his musical studies with both Maurice Ravel in France and Max Bruch in Berlin, gradually ironing out weaknesses in his composition, particularly the orchestration which he found so difficult.

Still regarded as a gifted amateur rather than a professional musician, by dogged perseverance he slowly gained a place in the musical establishment, and at the age of 25 he married Adeline Fisher, whom he had met when an undergraduate at Cambridge and who shared many of his interests. It was as he neared his thirties that he was gripped by a new and compelling enthusiasm for the folksongs which he declared were the true voice of English music, now in danger of becoming extinct. Scotland, Wales, and Ireland had different traditions and rhythms but, where music was concerned, English vernacular culture had been ignored and neglected for centuries.

Together with Cecil Sharp, a fellow enthusiast, and George Butterworth, he toured the country with his notebook, tracking down old men and women and persuading them to sing for him, and in this way collected hundreds of haunting ancient melodies that might otherwise have vanished for ever. One of his first orchestral works, *Norfolk Rhapsody,* which was based on folksongs acquired in this manner, was soon followed by the famous *Fantasia on a Theme of Thomas Tallis,* and many other successful ventures into different branches of musical creativity including opera, symphonies, and church music, in all of which the influence of folksongs is easily discerned.

Despite being a professed agnostic, Vaughan Williams worked for a time as an organist for a London parish where he described the choristers as louts and the vicar as 'quite mad'. He also accepted a commission to edit *The English Hymnal,* drawing on folksongs to replace the heavily sentimental Victorian music of *Hymns Ancient and Modern* and, where necessary, composing new tunes to fit the words. Ten years later he was to write a *Mass in G Minor* for the choir of Westminster Cathedral, commenting in his down-to-earth manner, 'There is no reason why an agnostic could not write a good Mass.'

Vaughan Williams's characteristic pragmatism stood him in good stead during the horrors of the First World War, for which he volunteered even though he had flat feet and, at the age of 42, was much older than the others with whom he served as a stretcher-bearer in Flanders and then, after 1916, at Salonika, providing medical help in the struggle against the German-supporting Turks.

The bleak *Pastoral Symphony* he wrote after hostilities ended had been forming in his mind throughout his military service, and is often seen as an elegy for the fallen, who included not only his brother-in-law Charles Fisher but also his great friend and fellow composer George Butterworth.

Though he had been a late developer and slow to achieve critical acclaim, during the inter-war years Vaughan Williams's output was impressive. Choral and orchestral works, songs, a ballet and opera, chamber music and further hymn tunes brought him increasingly to the forefront of the musical scene as audiences recognised and appreciated his unique talent for expressing what England made and what made England. Not only was his particular voice accepted, but it was beginning to be imitated by younger men. From the death of Elgar onwards, he was the country's most highly-regarded composer.

Yet his personal life was troubled. His wife Adeline had been so badly stricken with rheumatoid arthritis that she was confined to a wheelchair. Since she was unable to manage stairs, they moved to a bungalow near Dorking, and though honour and affection tethered RVW to her side, he was increasingly drawn to flirt with younger women.

In contrast to his heavy frame and tweedy, rumpled appearance, his letters reveal a quirky, almost skittish sense of humour. When the brilliant pianist Harriet Cohen asked him to write her a piano concerto, he jokingly charged her 'ten thousand kisses, to be paid off over the next years of meetings', and when Ursula Wood, a poet and drama student nearly forty years younger than him, wrote to tell him of her admiration for his ballet based on the book of *Job,* he was easily persuaded to take her out to lunch. Expecting the kind of frugal meal an impoverished musician might offer her, she was surprised to be taken to a gourmet restaurant, and more surprised still when, in the taxi back, Vaughan Williams enveloped her in a bear hug and kissed her enthusiastically.

'Well, I'm not used to this,' she exclaimed.

'You will be soon,' was his reply, and when she rang to thank him next morning, he rushed round to her house with his face only half-shaved.

Their blossoming affair revitalised him, and launched him into a new burst of creativity. He would never leave Adeline, he told Ursula frankly, but she would be 'the icing on the cake'. She became his constant companion, helped with his work and, after the death of her soldier husband, moved into the Dorking bungalow for weeks on end. Though she claimed to find Adeline alarming, she later described how the three of them would share a bedroom during the Blitz, with Ursula on the floor between the beds, holding Adeline's hand on one side and Ralph's on the other as the bombers roared overhead.

As the war he had long dreaded began to threaten Britain's very existence, Vaughan Williams – much too old now to fight – threw himself into the war effort. He grew vegetables and kept chickens, took in evacuees and found work for refugees escaping Nazism. His was the inspiration behind Dame Myra Hess's lunchtime recitals at the National Gallery, and he accepted the chairmanship of a Home Office committee considering the release of interned alien musicians, as well as the Council for the Encouragement of Music and the Arts, which later morphed into the Arts Council.

Meanwhile, he continued to work on his Fifth Symphony, which he conducted himself at the Proms in June 1943, but anyone who imagined that at the age of 71 his career was winding down was in for a surprise, for now a new field of musical creativity had engaged his enthusiasm. During the war a former pupil, Muir Mathieson, had persuaded him to write the score for the film *49th Parallel,* which he followed with music for several others, including *Scott of the Antarctic.*

Though he was always clumsy and impractical in ordinary life, in music there seemed to be nothing to which he could not turn his hand. Opera, Chamber, Band, Hymn, Orchestral – and the range of his work is astonishing. Once again after he had completed his strange, powerful Sixth Symphony at the age of 75, the public expected him to slow down, but on the contrary old age became one of his most productive periods.

After the death of his wife in 1951, he put his domestic affairs entirely in Ursula Wood's hands, and they married quietly in February 1953, after selling the Dorking bungalow and moving back to London. For years Adeline's disability had curtailed his freedom to travel, and now for the remaining years of his life he and Ursula regularly visited France, Italy and America.

In New York, which Vaughan Williams regarded as the most

beautiful city in the world, he lectured and worked on his Eighth Symphony; and then to confound those who considered his career as a composer to be near its end, wrote the hauntingly beautiful Ninth Symphony which was to be his last. It was performed at the Proms with Sir Malcolm Sargent conducting, in June 1958, and the moving sight of the 85-year-old composer, leaning heavily on his stick, climbing the steps to the platform to acknowledge the applause was long remembered by the cheering audience.

With half a dozen projects still awaiting completion, the Grand Old Man of English music died in harness a few months later, having triumphantly lived up to his own credo that 'Modernism and conservatism are irrelevant. What matters is to be true to oneself'.

Chapter Nine

REVISITING THE PAST

The Arts and Crafts Movement

As industrialisation gripped the nation in the nineteenth century, turning accepted work patterns on their heads and changing whole communities from self-employed craftsmen into mere factory workers, toiling in rows all day in noisy, grimy conditions, each person concentrated on producing just a single part of a manufactured article instead of the whole thing, nostalgia for the old days of artisan skills gave impetus to what became known as the Arts and Crafts Movement.

Though its inspiration and earliest proponents were the Pre-Raphaelite artists Edward Burne-Jones and Dante Gabriel Rossetti, themselves devotees of John Ruskin, and their ideals of beauty were heavily influenced by Tennyson's Arthurian romance *The Idylls of the King,* the Arts and Crafts Movement took a more practical turn through the involvement of the poet and architect William Morris. Nowhere did this new fashion last longer or gain more momentum than in Gloucestershire.

William Morris, who was born in 1834 in the Lea Valley in Hertfordshire, always believed that he belonged spiritually to another era. Mechanisation, industrialisation and standardisation were anathema to him. From his earliest years he was fascinated by the supposed pageantry and glamour of medieval life as portrayed in the *Waverley* novels of Sir Walter Scott, and as a child he was never happier than when riding his pony wearing the miniature suit of armour his father had had made for him, imagining himself a knight errant in search of damsels in distress to rescue in the wooded glades of Epping Forest.

He was educated at Marlborough College, where he got into trouble by leading a pupils' revolt against some imagined injustice; already his social conscience was well to the fore. At Exeter College, Oxford, it was natural that he should be drawn to the company of artistic, idealistic young men such as Swinburne and Burne-Jones, and make a hero of Ruskin, whose arguments for natural justice and equality they eagerly endorsed. The talented Pre-Raphaelite artist Dante Gabriel Rossetti, too, had a similar obsession with all things medieval, and this group, who named

William Morris: his most creative times were spent at Kelmscott, the enchanting Tudor manor house near Lechlade, Gloucestershire, which he rented with Dante Gabriel Rossetti.

themselves 'The Brothers', endlessly discussed the poetry, art, and architecture of the Age of Chivalry, endowing it with a glamour that soon undermined Morris's never-very-strong desire to take holy orders.

Abandoning his clerical studies, he began to write poetry which, if not actually copied, at least owed most of its inspiration to Tennyson and Chaucer. He was comfortably off, compared to most undergraduates, with no immediate need to earn a living when he left Oxford in 1855. Instead he and Burne-Jones embarked on a leisurely tour of the Gothic castles and cathedrals they admired, before Morris changed tack once more, making up his mind to study architecture. To this end – rather to his father's dismay – he took a job in the London office of George Edmund Street, and there found himself working alongside Philip Webb, already a promising young architect, who became a lifelong friend.

It was with Burne-Jones, however, that Morris shared rooms in Red Lion Square, and under his influence that he abandoned his plans to qualify as an architect and decided instead to devote himself to art.

But Art in what form? As his restless energy focused on one branch of creativity after another, Morris travelled to and fro between London and Oxford, in pursuit of the woman in whom he seemed to recognise his ideal of medieval beauty, the striking brunette Jenny Burden.

Jenny's background could hardly have been more different from his own. She was barely educated and had grown up in poverty, the daughter of a groom in a livery stable, who moved his family from one slum dwelling to another whenever he took a new job. At the time of Jenny's birth he was living in the passage which leads from New College lane to the Turf Tavern in Oxford, and the black-haired 'stunner' – who became the inspiration of the greatest Pre-Raphaelite artists – passed her childhood in the poor streets in and around Holywell and the Cornmarket.

What training she had was as a needlewoman, and she was earning her living as an embroiderer when a chance meeting with Rossetti and Burne-Jones led to her sitting to them as model for Guenevere in the murals they were creating for the Oxford Union. When she was introduced to their friend William Morris, he fell passionately in love at first sight. With her slim body and swanlike neck that looked too slender to support her astonishing mass of dark, waving hair, parted in the centre and looped up over each temple to frame her narrow face; with her thick, slanting eyebrows and small, sulky mouth, she had a strange, other-worldly beauty that perfectly represented his romantic Arthurian ideals.

Socially, she was not at all what William's father had hoped for, but she was astute enough to take advantage of the crash course in polite education that Morris arranged for her – an experiment adopted by Bernard Shaw for his play *Pygmalion* – and they were married two years later in 1859, when William was 25 and Jenny only 19 years old. A year later he commissioned his friend Philip Webb to design the famous Red House in Bexleyheath, south London, and with his friends set to with a will to furnish and decorate it in true medieval style, with tapestries, stained glass, and properly hand-crafted furniture.

The result, they all agreed, was a triumph, and they wanted to do it again. Thus was formed the grandly named Morris, Marshall, Faulkner and Company, whose founder members included Burne-Jones, Rossetti, Webb and Ford Madox Brown – but it was Morris who paid the bills.

At that happy, optimistic period, he also discovered his real forte: design. Wonderful rippling, intricate, repeating patterns of leaves, flowers, plants and fruit, birds and beasts flowed from his imagination to be translated on to wallpapers, fabrics, tapestries, textiles and the richly-decorated chapter headings and margins of books. They were indubitably designs inspired by Nature, but Nature refined and stylised into an ideal form. They were completely original, completely captivating, and they had a powerful influence on popular taste which they have never lost. It seemed Morris could turn his hand to designing and decorating anything or everything, and the firm flourished as fashionable London flocked to buy whatever it produced.

Personal life was less rosy, because the Morrises' marriage proved difficult. Despite the birth of two daughters, so ill-matched were William and Jenny's backgrounds that after the first heady

Rodmarton Manor – one of the last great houses to be built in Britain using only local materials and traditional methods of construction.

flush of romance, they struggled to establish a stable relationship. Similarly, the dashing, three-quarter-Italian Rossetti, whose long-term mistress was Elizabeth Siddal – another Pre-Raphaelite model in the same mould as Jenny, tall, long-necked and frail, with luxuriant coppery locks – faced the same problem of social incompatibility, though with a worse outcome. After a long-drawn-out engagement that lasted nearly a decade, they eventually married in 1859, only for poor Lizzie to die within two years from an overdose of morphia. Rossetti did not repine for long. A few months after his wife's untimely death, he transferred his affections first to the busty blonde Fanny Cornforth and then to Jenny Morris.

Despite his theoretical support for communal living and co-operative working, it was a heavy blow to William Morris to discover that his wife was having an affair with one of his best friends. Inevitably it strained their relationship, but – in the true spirit of chivalry – instead of reproaching the adulterous couple, Morris withdrew into a frenzy of work, designing textiles, writing poetry, and even embarking on the difficult self-imposed task of learning Icelandic, in order to translate the northern sagas into English.

He was also single-handedly battling with the costs of the company's business, and found the only time he could relax and recharge his creativity was during the periods he spent at Kelmscott, an enchanting Tudor manor house near Lechlade. It may seem curious that he rented this country hideaway jointly with Rossetti, but perhaps like King Arthur he hoped that the Lancelot/Guenevere relationship between his wife and friend would burn itself out – as, indeed, it eventually did. Meanwhile Morris spent much time travelling, leaving the lovers at Kelmscott to their own devices while he went walking in Italy with Swinburne as in their post-graduate days, and explored the wild wastes and wilder mythology of Iceland.

As six years dragged by, Rossetti became increasingly paranoid. Fuelled by chloral mixed with whisky, he used to sit on the manor wall at Kelmscott and glower menacingly at fishermen across the stream, or hurl abuse at them until local people complained, and in her husband's absence Jenny was forced to intervene. With Rossetti in the grip of a mental breakdown, she persuaded his family to remove him to Scotland, where he recovered enough to paint again, though he was never fully well and died ten years later of kidney failure.

Throughout this difficult period, Morris was becoming increasingly involved in Socialist politics, his conscience troubled by the growing disparity between rich and poor as the implementation of the industrial revolution led to mass unemployment among formerly self-sufficient craftsmen, tradesmen, and agricultural workers. His attitude to money was ambivalent. Although he had always taken full advantage of his own private income, he used often to complain that he was using his talents to 'minister to the swinish luxuries of the rich'.

Horrified by the wholesale destruction of ancient buildings in Victorian England, or their insensitive 'restoration' using new materials and techniques which made them, he claimed, historical forgeries, in 1877 he and Philip Webb founded The Society for the Protection of Ancient Buildings, which has over the past century and a half had an incalculable effect on preserving our rich heritage. Even today, the Society must be notified of all applications in England and Wales to demolish a listed building.

He was a tireless worker, both in the cause of a more equal society and as a champion of the decorative arts, and among the many budding architects and artists of the next generation inspired by his work and lectures was Charles Robert Ashbee, who became a pivotal figure in the Arts and Crafts Movement.

In 1887, Ashbee founded the Guild of Handicrafts in Whitechapel, dedicated to reviving craft skills among the workers of East London. When this function was undercut financially by the free classes offered by the London County Council, Ashbee moved his Guild to Elm Tree House at Chipping Campden in the Cotswolds, where Morris's ideal of a rural community sustained by traditional crafts in local workshops might be more accurately realised.

He was particularly talented as a silversmith, and his beautifully simple, exquisitely crafted jewellery, belt buckles and tableware are still eagerly sought-after, but they were too expensive to sustain a regular market, and after twenty years of gradually falling sales, the Guild had to be disbanded. By then, however, the Arts and Crafts Movement had taken on a new lease of life under the direction of three young architect-designers: the brothers Ernest and Sidney Barnsley, who came from Birmingham, and Leicester-born Ernest Gimson.

Drawn by the beauty of Cotswold stone and the great tradition of vernacular architecture in Gloucestershire, where the buildings look as if they have grown out of the soil, so perfectly do they blend with their surroundings, this talented trio decided to live near Cirencester. Impressed with their work, Lord Bathurst allowed them to rent nearby Pinbury Park on a repairing lease, which gave them the perfect springboard from which to launch their campaign to revive old building techniques and furniture-making crafts which were in danger of dying out.

Ernest and his family lived at one end of the house, with a communal workshop connecting it to the cottages which his brother Sidney and Ernest Gimson converted into living quarters. The elder Barnsley brother was a big, bluff, good-looking man who loved good food and good company, while Sidney, his junior by two years and always jocularly referred to as 'the Boy,' was an austere and solitary character who kept social life to a minimum.

In contrast Gimson was friendly and easy-going, popular with all classes, and a tremendous walker whose long legs covered the surrounding hills and valleys with great strides as he indulged his interest in natural history during his hours away from the drawing-board. He was fascinated by local folklore, and in the country dances and old songs which Cecil Sharp and Ralph Vaughan Williams were rescuing from oblivion just as Gimson and his friends were reviving traditional crafts before they died out.

When the newly married Lord Bathurst took the beautifully restored Pinbury Park back for his own use in 1902, in exchange for them giving up their lease he generously gave both Barnsley brothers and Gimson land at Sapperton on which to build their own cottages at his expense, which they did using local materials, traditional building methods, and locally-grown timber.

Lord Bathurst had also commissioned them to restore nearby Daneway House, and from 1902 to 1919, the three used the High Building – the former Great Hall – as a showroom to display Gimson's furniture, while the converted stables served as workshop and studio. It was all beautifully self-contained.

The biggest commission of all, which led to the building of what may be regarded as Edward Barnsley's masterpiece – came from local landowner and successful stockbroker Claud Biddulph and his wife Margaret. Though his family roots were in Herefordshire, Claud had been given 500 acres at Rodmarton, near Sapperton, in 1894, and the Biddulphs moved to Gloucestershire on the eve of the First World War, primarily for sporting purposes. However, their interest in shooting and hunting soon diminished when they met the Barnsleys and became fascinated with the project of building an entirely new home according to the best principles of the Arts and Crafts Movement.

A very big home, too. Many-gabled Rodmarton Manor is one of the last great houses built in Britain in which all the materials used in construction and furnishing were not only found locally, but worked using traditional techniques. Stone came from a nearby quarry and was transported to the site on horse-drawn carts. Timber was grown on the estate, and planks were sawn in a pit by hand, rather than with a labour-saving circular saw, and although the Biddulphs agreed to the installation of electric light, in nearly every way they stuck to the building methods of pre-industrial Britain.

When the Biddulphs moved in, they kept the large central

rooms and great hall for the use of the local community, and confined their own living quarters to the east end of the house. Craft classes, puppet shows, poetry readings and musical evenings were held in what soon became a cultural hub for people living round about.

Margaret Biddulph had trained at a horticultural college, and the garden at Rodmarton was her particular interest. Divided into a series of interconnecting 'rooms', it was a forerunner of many modern designs and, though frequently in conflict with her equally strong-willed head gardener, William Scrubey, Mrs Biddulph created a beautiful and productive garden that is still cherished by her grandson today.

The success of the Sapperton Group attracted many like-minded apprentices in carpentry and cabinet-making, and artists in metal, plaster, and stonework to the area, until there was a flourishing colony of craftsmen living in and around Cirencester. Though Gimson and the Barnsley brothers all died relatively young, and are buried in Sapperton churchyard under the yews by the entrance gate, their spirit lives on in the houses and cottages they designed and built, the furniture, tapestries and metalwork they created and, above all, in the traditional crafts they had re-invigorated, while adhering faithfully to William Morris's philosophy that happiness and harmony lay in having 'nothing in your house that you do not know to be useful or believe to be beautiful'.

Chapter Ten

CONCORDE

The great one-off

Whether you regard the Anglo-French supersonic commercial passenger aircraft as a triumph of international co-operation and design or the most disastrous investment a British government has made since the Second World War, Concorde is indissolubly linked to its starting and eventual last resting-place at Filton, in south Gloucestershire, where fighters and bombers including the Blenheim, Beaufort, Beaufighter and Brigand had been produced during the Second World War. The runway had been extended to accommodate the mighty Bristol Brabazon, which made it a suitable site for testing a supersonic passenger plane the like of which had never been seen before.

Instantly recognisable by its delta wings and sleek, predatory neck, as well as its ear-splitting noise, Concorde aroused equally strong feelings of admiration and antipathy in those who followed its progress from drawing-board to museum piece over forty turbulent years.

Pilots loved it. 'Wizard' was the verdict of Brian Trubshaw, the test pilot at the controls on Concorde's maiden flight from Filton to Fairford, while Brian Calvert, who regularly flew the plane across the Atlantic, praised its stability and precision, comparing it to a well-schooled racehorse.

But... 'A commercial disaster', was the conclusion of Lord Rothschild's think-tank, the Central Policy Review Staff.

They were all correct. Concorde was beautiful, futuristic, an astonishing feat of aerodynamic engineering, but very, very expensive and tremendously noisy.

Residents of Bristol were less than enthusiastic when the aircraft first went into service. Gates and traffic lights had to be installed to close off the A38 when it was about to take off from Filton, and complaints from people living near Heathrow escalated immediately. A study by the Greater London Council pointed out that the plane's characteristic noise 'footprint' affected far more people than that of other aircraft. New York Port Authority banned it at first, since noise take-off level exceeded 112 Perceived Noise Decibels, enough to damage human hearing.

Yet no one could question Concorde's amazing capabilities. At Mach 2, twice the speed of sound, it was flying faster than a bullet. Passengers who were wafted from one side of the Atlantic to the other in three hours were lavish with their praise, but though the seats were comfortable, some found the narrow fuselage claustrophobic, and the flexing wings attracted nervous glances. It was also difficult to talk over the noise. The real trouble was that it carried very few travellers on each flight. Although optimistic forecasts had claimed it would be possible to transport 150 people at a time, on long-haul flights the plane was operating at the limits of its capabilities, and whole rows of seats were often roped off to save weight. It was also extremely expensive, costing roughly five times as much to fly a passenger supersonically as on a conventional flight.

So how did such an money-guzzling white elephant ever get off the ground?

The Concorde project was jolted into being after the disastrous

Half British, half French, Concorde was instantly recognisable by its delta wings and sleek, predatory neck, as well as its ear-splitting noise.

explosion of two Comets over the Mediterranean in 1954, killing all on board, and the subsequent grounding of Comets for two years. By the time they were judged fit to fly again, the American Boeing 707 and DC-8 had captured most of the world's airline market and, rather than compete with the Americans on this ground, Britain's technological experts at Farnborough called for research into a supersonic passenger plane, a step into the future that would put British aviation ahead of all other nations.

Morien Morgan, then Farnborough's deputy director, was an enthusiastic promoter of the plan. Such a plane would, he said, 'enable Britain to look America firmly in the eye again'. Brushing aside the doubts of manufacturers and the opposition of the Treasury, which had already been obliged to underwrite too many of the aviation industry's mistakes, in 1956 he convened a meeting known as the Supersonic Transport Aircraft Committee, or STAC, to examine the possibility of designing a supersonic airliner.

After various proposals were dismissed as non-starters, STAC seized on the cautious suggestion by Dietrich Kuchemann, a German aerodynamic expert for whose services both America and Britain had competed at the end of the War, that a very thin delta-winged supersonic passenger plane was, as he put it, 'just possible'.

That qualifying 'just' was airbrushed out of the enthusiastic report from STAC which was sent to the Ministry's controller of aircraft in 1959. Nor was the proposal debated in Parliament until December 1962, a month *after* an Anglo-French treaty had committed Britain to the project without an escape clause. Once the treaty was signed there was no possibility of withdrawal.

It is nothing new for government-funded prestige projects to over-run estimated costs, nor for politicians to be economical with the truth, but in the case of Concorde the discrepancy between forecasts and reality was truly startling, for the very good reason that the entire project was never properly costed in advance.

According to Herr Kuchemann himself, the head of Farnborough's aerodynamic department, Philip Hufton, based the figures on what he thought the politicians would stand. 'In the whole STAC report,' said Kuchemann, shortly before his death in 1976, 'those estimates are the only thing that is rubbish. I have a very bad conscience about that.'

Even relying on the most optimistic figures for costs and sales of a supersonic airliner, it was clear from the start that if Britain was to go ahead with the project it would need a partner with whom to share the expense. A succession of Europhile aviation ministers, most of whom had been disappointed by Britain's failure to join the EEC, (European Economic Community, as the European Union was then called) made exploratory overtures to several countries, but only France, eager as ever to do the Americans in the eye, looked likely to join the project.

Duncan Sandys, then the minister, presented the scheme to Parliament, arguing that without a supersonic passenger plane, Britain could no longer claim to be a power in world aviation, and his successor Peter Thorneycroft was urged to follow the same line by his parliamentary secretary, Geoffrey Rippon, who chaired the steering committee determined to see the supersonic project through.

Rippon regarded the Treasury mandarins with disdain, dismissing them as narrowly self-interested and lacking in vision. His strategy was to keep the Treasury in the dark concerning costs until a deal with the French had been finalised and it would be impossible for Britain to withdraw. To this end he gave the French, in 1960, a copy of the confidential STAC report, even though it was still secret in Britain and was to remain so for over a decade. Once they had seen the aerodynamic secret of Concorde, the French agreed to join the project as an equal partner, and it was they who insisted that the name was spelt in the French way with a final 'e'.

Julian Amery, the strongly pro-European minister who eventually signed the treaty, was jubilant, expecting such evidence of co-operation to secure General de Gaulle's approval for Britain's bid to join the Common Market (as the EEC had become), but his hopes were dashed by the General's unequivocal '*Non*' only six weeks later.

Like it or not, however, Britain was now firmly locked into the Concorde project, from which neither country could withdraw without incurring all the development costs borne by both countries. Technical discussions fraught with confusion about specifications for airframe and engines continued for the next five years between the Bristol-based British Aircraft Corporation (BAC) and Sud-Aviation of Toulouse. Much of the difficulty arose from the fact that each company had a different vision of what they were aiming at. BAC wanted to fly the Atlantic, while Sud-Aviation was more drawn to medium-range flights.

Battling for the engine-building contract were Rolls-Royce and Bristol-Siddeley, and it was largely because Rolls-Royce acknowledged the problem that engine noise was likely to cause with the New York authorities that it lost out to the rival firm. The model eventually chosen was the Olympus, which had been used in the RAF Canberra as far back as 1952, and all attempts to render it less noisy were negated by the airframe builders' continual demands for more power.

As the long-drawn-out series of test flights zoomed across the Cotswolds out of Filton and Fairford, Gloucestershire people grew used to seeing the strange triangular shape pass overhead. Some likened it to a beautiful bird, slender and feminine. Others thought it resembled a paper dart, while cynics saw it as a prehistoric monster with curious eating habits, whose favourite food was taxpayers' money.

At Farnborough, two prototypes were installed in huge rigs which could heat or cool the structure to extreme temperatures. Hydraulic jacks tortured it meanwhile with stresses designed to seek out any hint of metal fatigue. The windows and windshield were tested by firing dead chickens at them.

Both Governments had ordered a complete amalgamation of responsibilities between the English and French companies. Thus the engines were made in England, but the intakes in France. Filton made the nose and tail; Toulouse constructed the wings and centre-fuselage. In the production run, each of the two factories assembled alternate aircraft.

Considering that the English factory was using imperial

measurements and the French metric ones, it is astonishing that no irreversible mistakes had crept into the test models by the time 001, the French Concorde, made its maiden flight from Toulouse in March, 1969, and under intense scrutiny from the world press, flew for 42 minutes at an airspeed of 250 knots.

In April, it was the turn of 002, Britain's version, to take off from Filton with Brian Trubshaw in command. The flight was by no means trouble-free. First the captain's airspeed indicator appeared unreliable, showing a warning flag which was not replicated on the co-pilot's instrument; then both radio altimeters failed, obliging Trubshaw to land at Fairford purely by eye.

Longer and faster test flights followed, while possible routes were considered and explored. Stories in the press about the dangerous effects of 'sonic boom' kept public interest alert. Cows were alleged to have aborted and horses bolted, and the volleys of complaints that bombarded BAC even on days when Concorde had not flown ended any hopes of supersonic flight over Britain. Rough runways in Athens and very cold air in Teheran brought their own hazards, but it was always excessive noise that engendered most opposition from those on the ground.

Though the British authorities ducked the noise problem by exempting Concorde from the limits imposed on other aircraft at Heathrow, the New York Port Authority was less amenable and much negotiation was required before obtaining permission to land there. Nor was the question of payload easy to resolve. As new snags had emerged at each stage of design and extra safety equipment was introduced, ever lower sank the number of passengers it was deemed safe to carry long-haul. The optimistic initial estimate of 150 became 130, then 100 to New York but only 80 to Washington, two hundred miles farther away. Flying from Bahrain posed special difficulty because of the heat at take-off, and the number was limited to 70.

Hopes that Concorde would prove popular with other

airlines were also disappointed. Far from queuing to buy the supersonic marvel, one national carrier after another decided against it. At the beginning of the age of mass-tourism and growing environmental awareness, when airlines knew they were soon going to require larger, quieter, more economical passenger planes, a speedbird for the elite, such as Concorde, was bucking the market trend. Since they had failed to hold pre-production design consultations with interested companies which might have enticed them to take options which would lead to sales, the Anglo-French team, chivvied by their governments, found they had built a wonderful airliner which no one actually wanted. Both Pan Am and TWA withdrew their tentative options, and British Airways and Air France were the only companies actually to buy the heavily-subsidised plane. Instead of the projected fleet of 200 flying all over the world, only 16 were ever built.

So died an ambitious dream of pulling off a spectacular coup that would capture the world airline market and put Britain once again at the forefront of aviation history. As usual, the devil was in the detail, and detail was the last thing that politicians like Morien Morgan and Duncan Sandys were interested in.

Despite being too noisy, too cramped, and way too expensive, Concorde was much praised for its reliability during the two decades in which it was in service, and its distinctive appearance was a source of national pride. It was a terrible blow when in July, 2000, an Air France Concorde crashed in Paris just after take-off, killing 109 passengers and four people on the ground, and the whole fleet was immediately grounded for a year.

After £17 million had been spent on safety improvements, the aircraft resumed commercial flying, but the accident had been the first in a series of minor problems. A year later part of a tail rudder fell off, then on different occasions an engine failure which caused a mid-air explosion frightened the passengers; cracks appeared in windows; an engine power surge led to a flight being aborted, and on one occasion at least take-off was abandoned after a computer glitch.

Eventually, in April 2003, BA and Air France announced that the aircraft would be taken out of service for good, and the dramatic footage of Concorde 216, last of the line, zooming over the Clifton suspension bridge on its final flight home to Filton will long remain in the mind's eye of many Bristolians.

There in Filton Concorde remains, an engineering triumph that never managed to fulfil its promise, waiting for money – yet again! – to be raised for a worthy museum to house it.

Chapter Eleven

SPORTING AND FARMING LIFE

Gold Cup Greats

The Cheltenham Gold Cup, which was first run at Prestbury Park in 1924, quickly established itself as the supreme test of the staying steeplechaser at level weights. The Aintree fences may look more formidable, but the Grand National is a handicap in which luck, weight, weather and going are bound to play a more important part than on a park course, where the runners are evenly matched and must rely solely on their speed, courage, and jumping ability; and with its 22 fences to be jumped over 3 miles 2 furlongs, plus a long, draining, uphill finish, the Cheltenham Gold Cup is considered the most prestigious of all National Hunt events.

Outstanding among the many winners of this gruelling race was the heroic Golden Miller, whose record of five consecutive Gold Cups between the years 1932 to 1936 has never been beaten. His origins were curious. In 1914 a Dublin businessman named Julius Solomon who knew nothing about bloodstock decided nonetheless to buy a brood mare, but so little interest did he take in the selection that he sat in his car and let his chauffeur choose one from a farmer named James Nugent. For one hundred pounds Mr Solomon became the owner of a mare named Miller's Pride,

Golden Miller holds the record for five consecutive Cheltenham Gold Cup wins, between the years 1932 and 1936.

which he sent to board with a breeder named Laurence Geraghty, in Co. Meath.

When war broke out, Mr Solomon lost interest in his mare, whom Mr Geraghty treated as his own and from whom he bred several foals. In 1926 Miller's Pride was covered by a stallion named Goldcourt, whose stud fee was only 5 guineas, but the colt foal she produced was a cut above all his siblings, and he was sold as a yearling at Ballsbridge for an impressive thousand guineas.

As a five-year-old, now owned by the Hon Dorothy Paget, the rich, reclusive, and deeply eccentric daughter of Lord Queensborough, and trained by Basil Briscoe, he seemed too inexperienced to take on horses of the calibre of the Grand National winner Grakle, but in the Gold Cup several horses fell and Grakle was hampered, and 'The Miller' won comfortably by four lengths, a pattern he repeated in the following four years.

A long-striding horse with a low action, who jumped off his forehand and was inclined to be idle, he never made spectacular leaps but had bottomless stamina. Nor was he always partnered by the same jockey. On the contrary, in the course of his career he had seventeen different jockeys, fifteen pros and two amateurs,

The Cheltenham Gold Cup: the supreme test of the staying steeple-chaser at level weights.

and won twenty-nine races, including the Grand National.

As a seven-times winning owner, Dorothy Paget also still holds the Cheltenham Gold Cup record. Huge and unmistakable in her long, shapeless blue coat, with an unflattering beret clamped to uncompromisingly straight hair, and a large pale face devoid of make-up, she was nevertheless a shrewd and knowledgeable judge of a racehorse, though often a trial to the patience of her trainers. Only Charlie Rogers in Ireland managed to retain his post as her stud manager and trainer for more than 20 years.

She was very rich and placed enormous bets, and had an appetite to match, eating prodigiously and staying up most of the night. It was hardly surprising that she died of a heart attack at the age of 54, but the money she had ploughed into National Hunt racing had given the sport a welcome boost in the lean post-war period, and she was much mourned.

Although Pat Taaffe still holds the jockeys' record for four

Gold Cup wins, few racing people would not agree that Fred Winter, who dominated National Hunt racing between 1947 and 1964 as a jockey, and thereafter for many years as a trainer, was the king of Cheltenham races.

A small, dark, neat-featured man of few words, with an unquenchable will to win, Winter won a total of 923 races – 45 of them at Cheltenham – and was four times Champion Jockey, winning two Cheltenham Gold Cups on Saffron Tartan and on Mandarin.

On Mandarin, too, he achieved the most difficult feat of his career, steering his horse round the figure-8 course of the Grand Steeplechase de Paris at Auteuil entirely by legs and balance after the bit broke in the horse's mouth at the fourth of thirty cross-country fences – and bringing him home to win.

After retiring as a jockey, he set up as a trainer with only five horses, but was soon turning out winners again from his yard in the Cotswolds. Both Jay Trump and Anglo won the Grand National, and Midnight Court the Cheltenham Gold Cup, among many other successes, and in 1963 Fred Winter was awarded the CBE for services to National Hunt racing.

Great horses a-plenty have won Cheltenham's Gold Cup – in fact by definition the winner has to be an outstanding athlete – but few are as famous as Anne, Duchess of Westminster's bay Arkle, described by a racing journalist as 'a freak of nature', so utterly did he demolish the opposition in one race after another. First time out at Cheltenham, he won his race by twenty lengths, and went on to take three consecutive Gold Cups as well as a wide variety of valuable handicaps both in Britain and Ireland. When he won the Irish Grand National he was carrying *two and a half stone* more than his rivals – an extraordinary feat.

At the height of his fame, it was said that a letter addressed to 'Himself, Ireland', would be delivered to Arkle's stable in Tom Dreaper's yard, and his skeleton has been preserved in the museum of the National Stud in Co Kildare, as the relic of the greatest steeplechaser of all time.

Arkle may have been the greatest, but in the hearts of the racing public few can rival Desert Orchid, the glorious grey who carried all before him in the 1990s, and died full of honours at the grand old age of 27.

Desert Orchid, the glorious grey who carried all before him in the 1990s, and died full of honours at the grand old age of 27.

'Dessie' – as he was familiarly known – looked more like a middleweight show hunter than a racehorse, burly and muscular, with a handsome topline and beautifully chiselled head. His career got off to a bad start when he fell in his first hurdle race and took a worryingly long time to rise again; but when switched to fences he was soon in his element, being a spectacular jumper who made very few mistakes. Because of his tendency to jump to the right when tiring, he was happier on a right-handed course like

Kempton, where he won four consecutive King George VI stakes, than on left-handed courses such as Aintree and Cheltenham. For this reason his owner, Richard Burridge, did not enter him in the Grand National, but his right-handed tendency did not prevent him winning the Cheltenham Gold Cup in muddy conditions and driving rain, in what *Racing Post* called 'the race of the century'.

Dessie was a showman, too, dancing and prancing to delight the crowds when, after his retirement from the racecourse, he made guest appearances at many different sporting events and raised large sums for charity.

Cottage Rake and Best Mate were three-times winners, while L'Escargot and Kauto Star won it twice each: the Gold Cup has many four-legged greats and is certain to produce many more, though the record that will surely remain unbroken is trainer Michael Dickinson's achievement in 1983 when he trained all five of the first horses past the post.

Timed as it is to coincide with St Patrick's Day (March 17th) the Cheltenham Spring Festival always attracts huge crowds of Irish racegoers with wallets bulging, boundless enthusiasm, and apparently unquenchable thirst as they cheer on the cream of their 'chasers and hurdlers competing at the Festival, notably in the Champion Hurdle, the Queen Elizabeth Champion Chase and, of course, the Gold Cup itself. The deafening roar that greets an Irish winner returning to the enclosure is another tradition that gives Gold Cup Day its unique atmosphere.

The Badminton Horse Trials

It was the poor showing of the British equestrian team in the London Olympics of 1948, when the show-jumping bronze won by Colonel Harry Llewellyn on his handsome bay, Foxhunter, was the only medal awarded to a British rider, which prompted the tenth Duke of Beaufort to offer to give much-needed experience to the national team by holding an annual three-day event on his estate at Badminton in Gloucestershire. It was a brilliant idea and, since then, team and individual gold medals in abundance have been won by British riders, both in the European Championships and the Olympic Games.

Badminton House, in whose hall the game of badminton was first played, is a large handsome mansion dating from 1682, with magnificent stables and outbuildings, almost a village in itself. The north front has a fine Palladian facade surmounted by two cupolas, the work of William Kent, and the ancient turf of the extensive park around it, laid out by 'Capability' Brown, makes perfect galloping ground. There are a multitude of ways of jumping into and out of the ornamental lake in front of the house, and avenues of noble trees radiate out to the gate lodges on the edge of the park. There are watercourses and hedges and even farmyard walls that an inventive course-builder can incorporate into a cross-country course. All in all it is a perfect setting for horse trials.

From the modest beginning in 1949, when 22 horses competed and spectators roamed freely on a cross-country course marked out with binder-twine for a first prize of £150 (while the whole event made a profit of £6,) the Badminton Horse Trials have expanded into the biggest and most spectacular equestrian three-day event in the world, the one every horse-mad teenager dreams of winning. Yet despite the enormous growth of organisation, sophistication, and – inevitably – commercialisation, the basic format of three disciplines for the competing horses remains the same: first dressage, to demonstrate obedience, flexibility, and correct paces; next cross-country for speed, courage, and endurance; and the final showjumping phase, which proves that despite the exertions of the previous days, the horse is still fit enough to jump accurately round a fair-sized, twisting course.

For the first ten years, the dressage phase took place on the old cricket ground in front of the house, with spectators sitting on straw bales, but in 1959, after torrential rain which turned the park into a sea of mud, both the trade stands and the dressage and showjumping arena were moved to their present sites, and a proper grandstand was built to accommodate the ever-growing crowds of spectators.

Rules and qualification requirements became stricter, too. Though the first winner, Golden Willow, was only five years old, horses must nowadays be seven or more, with the oldest winner to date being Horton Point, aged 16. In order to qualify for entry to this top-grade, four-star event, horse and rider must amass a minimum number of points from other events, a process which may take several years. After this long and complicated build-up, there can be few moments more heartbreaking for a competitor than to have his or her horse rejected – 'spun,' as they call it – by the veterinary committee that inspects all the entrants the evening before the trials begin.

The inspection is a solemn ritual, for so much hangs on the vets' verdict. One after another, the super-fit horses are brought out of their luxurious quarters in the Badminton stableyard, and trotted up to and away from the panel of vets, and there is many an anxious glance from the rider running beside his or her animal before a voice announces whether it has passed or failed.

Next morning the crowds begin to arrive and the huge grass parking area quickly fills with every kind of vehicle, complete with passengers, dogs, and picnics. Those who have come to watch horses hurry towards the dressage arena enclosed by semi-covered grandstands while a surprisingly large proportion, who have come mainly for the shopping, head directly for the delights of a temporary tented village and its tempting rows of stalls. There you can buy goods ranging from a luxury horse-lorry to an ironing-board cover. Gourmet foods, jewellery, high fashion or kitsch – it is a savvy shopper's dream, and on the first morning the displays are fresh, the merchandise new and enticing. During the four days of the Badminton Horse Trials, some small businesses make half their yearly profits, and there is always a waiting list for a pitch in the Village.

Within the dressage arena, those interested in watching horses sit silently enthralled as one competitor after another goes through the sedate, carefully calibrated movements of a moderately difficult dressage test. Nothing fancy: no piaffe or levade, just walk, trot, canter at medium or extended paces, rein back, counter-canter, flying-change – with each movement awarded a mark by three different judges. This phase of the event continues for two days, and has a powerful influence on the final result, since it is rare for a horse with poor dressage marks to finish in the first ten.

Cross-country day brings more dramatic action – plus the bulk of the crowds, eager to witness at first-hand the thrills and spills. The endurance test begins with a long warm-up of several miles at a good round trot along tracks through the estate's extensive woodland, followed by a quick veterinary check and rest while the horse's mouth is washed out and his legs, chest and belly smeared with thick grease which, in the event of a fall, will help him slide harmlessly over the obstacle. That, at least, is the theory. Then comes the countdown, shouts of, 'Good luck!' and they are off to face the 30-odd daunting obstacles designed – as long-term course builder and Badminton trials director Colonel Frank Weldon put it – 'to frighten the life out of the riders without hurting the horses.'

Mary King riding Imperial Cavalier at the 2010 Badminton Horse Trials

To the eye of a spectator, the fences often look unjumpable. Massive timber, huge drops and leaps into water or up on to steps topped by narrow stiles; twisting combination fences where only the very corners can be jumped in a straight line; jumps over flower-decked pick-up trucks, or boats, or through enormous life-belts... The course-builder's invention knows no bounds, and although there are often alternative routes over a fence where the straight option looks too chancy, the easier route always costs precious extra seconds.

Yet so brave and athletic are the horses, so accurate and skilful their riders, that they soar over these formidable obstacles with apparent ease, and falls are comparatively rare. Experience is the key, and the same riders end up in the money year after year.

Both before and after her marriage, Lucinda Prior-Palmer (who became Lucinda Green), dominated Badminton Horse Trials in the 1970s and '80s, winning an astonishing six times. As well as being an outstanding rider, Lucinda seemed to possess a special *joie de vivre* which she could communicate to her mount, and all six of her winning horses looked as if they were enjoying themselves as much as she was.

Ever since 1952, when women were first allowed to enter, they have shown a particular flair for eventing, especially since the earlier requirement to carry twelve and a half stone was reduced in 1996 to eleven stone, which made it easier for smaller horses. So small, indeed, was one competitor's mount that, faced with a bridge to jump in a sunken ditch, he simply ducked underneath it, rider and all. Since no one had envisaged such a manoeuvre, they incurred no penalty, but the following year the rules were changed to insist that horses went *over* every fence!

By the end of the cross-country phase, the leading horses and riders are often within very few marks of one another, so the final day's showjumping can present a real cliffhanger, with nothing but a single fence down or an unexpected clear round enough to determine the winning order.

The needle-drop silence as the leaders jump, in reverse order, the course of flimsy coloured poles, so different from the massive fixed fences of the previous day, and the gasps of elation or disappointment from the crowd, bear witness to the tension, but it is one of the great strengths of eventing at the highest level that a sporting spirit prevails and competitors are unusually supportive of one another. Horses are unpredictable, and all riders know from experience that one day you may be collecting a trophy and £60,000, and a week later find yourself plunging head first into an icy lake when your mount takes a dislike to the water jump.

Anyone competing at this level of eventing has learnt long ago how frequently pride goes before a (very literal and often painful) fall. It takes a special courage to ride round a cross-country course of such size and complexity, and every one of those who manages to complete the Badminton Horse Trials thoroughly deserves the commemorative Armada dish with which he or she is presented.

Gloucester Old Spot Pigs

Easily recognised by the bold black splodges on a their thickly-bristled white skin and long floppy ears reaching down to their quizzical, upturned snouts, these charming pigs were traditionally kept to graze orchards and clear up windfalls on the Berkeley Vale's many dairy farms, and were fattened on the whey produced from butter-making.

Big, sturdy, full-bodied pigs with placid, laid-back natures, they are generally easy to handle, though a full-grown sow with her trotters on the door of her pen, squealing and slavering for her breakfast, is guaranteed to make the strongest man hurry up with the bucket of feed-nuts.

Spotted pigs are often seen in old paintings of rural scenes,

Gloucester Old Spot sow: a big, sturdy, full-bodied pig with a laid-back nature and a keen appetite for windfall apples.

which gives rise to the claim that the breed is of some antiquity, and certainly the GOS has been pure bred for the past hundred years. It is popular nowadays with specialist butchers who value the rich, slow-matured pork and bacon, and the breed has recently been awarded Protected Status by the European Union, along with Stilton and Cheddar cheese and Melton Mowbray pork pies.

The breed is also honoured with royal connections. Prince Charles keeps a small herd of Old Spots at his farm at Highgrove, near Tetbury, and the Princess Royal, who lives near Avening, is Patron of the Gloucestershire Old Spots Pig Breeders' Club; yet forty years ago when Continental breeds like the Danish Landrace were all the rage, Old Spots fell so far out of public favour that very few pure-breds remained. At that low point consumers accused them of being too fatty, and butchers complained that the spots made cleaning the carcases difficult.

It was largely thanks to the energy and dedication of George Styles, respectfully known among Old Spot *aficionados* as the Grandfather of the Breed, that numbers have now built up to the point where it is numerically the largest pedigree pig in the Rare Breeds Survival Trust, which monitors the most endangered varieties of farm animals. So with interest in high-quality local food increasing year on year, prospects for the Gloucester Old Spot look set fair for another hundred years at least.

Gloucester Cattle

A familiar sight in the Cotswold hills and Severn Vale since at least the 13th century, these large, handsome, dark-brown cows, with their wide-spaced, upward-sweeping white horns and the characteristic white 'finching' stripe running the length of back and tail, are more than a dual-purpose breed. Real multi-taskers, with co-operative, adaptable natures, they have supplied generations of Gloucestershire farming families with milk and meat as well as teams of oxen to till the fields. The medical world's most famous cow, Blossom, from whom Dr Jenner developed his cowpox vaccine was, naturally, a Gloucester, as proved by the appearance of all seven of the hides purporting to have belonged to her.

The cattle are hardy, industrious foragers, happy to live out all year round in their thick winter coats, and very well suited to any extensive system of parkland management, or keeping down scrub in conservation areas.

Although the amount of milk they produce is modest in commercial dairying terms — an average of 850 gallons in a lactation compared to the 1400-plus of heavy yielders like Friesian-Holsteins — it is milk of a special quality, high in protein and butterfat with particularly small globules, which make it perfect for cheese-making. Both the world-famous Single Gloucester and that gourmet's favourite Stinking Bishop must be made from the milk of Gloucester Cattle, (although it is permissible to use other milk for the less recherché Double Gloucester.)

Another advantage is that Gloucester cattle have a flat lactation curve — just what you want in a house-cow, when it is equally inconvenient to be flooded with milk after calving or reduced to a trickle towards the end of the lactation. The Gloucester cow goes on producing much the same amount week after week until

Gloucester cattle at summer pasture: handsome, dark-brown cows with wide-spaced, upward-sweeping horns and the characteristic white 'finching' stripe running the length of back and tail.

dried off, and this is naturally easier on her own metabolism than the extravagant highs and lows of commercial dairy breeds. She therefore has an enviable reputation for longevity, and it is common enough for her productive life to span 12-15 years rather than the 9-12 of the highest yielding breeds.

Despite all these virtues the popularity of Gloucester cattle declined from its high point in the 1750s, when they could be found from Devon to Essex, to just one substantial herd in 1972. Part of the reason was the introduction of new, specialised breeds both for milk-production and beef, and the development of intensive agricultural systems, and part the large post-war increase in arable farming, which resulted in the loss of much grassland.

It was at this low point in its fortunes, when the last remaining pedigree herd was dispersed at a sale, that the breed seemed destined for extinction. But at the last minute a group of five enthusiasts agreed to revive the Gloucester Cattle Society, setting up a register of pure-bred animals and accepting on to it only those which conformed to a pre-determined standard of looks, colouring and performance.

Such has been their success that there are now over 700 registered cows, but the breed is still classified as Endangered, and closely monitored by the Rare Breeds Survival Trust's watch list. It is hoped that, with organic farming increasing in popularity and the special qualities of slow-maturing dual-purpose animals being more generally recognised, Gloucester Cattle will eventually regain their earlier status in the county where they originated.

Khaki Campbell ducks – descendants of the doughty Mrs Campbell's cross-breeding experiments at Uley.

Khaki Campbell Ducks

Long before scientists in their laboratories began to manipulate genetic material in the hope of creating bigger, better, more productive farm animals, Mrs Adele Campbell, who lived in the Gloucestershire village of Uley at the end of the 19th century, conducted her own cross-breeding experiment.

She was, it is said, a tough old bird herself, tall and red-faced, with a habit of shouting at her neighbours, who in turn attributed her florid complexion to a fondness for the bottle. Her husband Arthur, a doctor with philanthropic tendencies, who treated poor patients free, secured his own freedom by retreating to a bungalow in Sussex when he retired, but his wife stayed on in Uley, breeding ducks.

Her aim was to increase the egg-laying power of her flock, and by first crossing a big heavy-bodied Rouen duck with one of her light-boned, vertical-gaited Indian Runners and then adding a wild mallard to the mix for extra hardiness, she managed to produce a medium-sized utility duck with astonishing egg-laying powers, which she proudly presented to the world in 1898.

Asked what the new breed was called, she replied, 'A Campbell', and when further crossings with Pencilled Runners produced offspring that were almost entirely brown, she amended the name to 'Khaki Campbell' and this is how it is now known all over the world.

Though the drakes have greeny-bronze heads and bright orange bills to set off their brown, pencil-streaked plumage, the ducks are uniformly pencil-streaked brown, with dark eyes and slate-coloured bills. They may not be the most handsome ducks in the world, but they are certainly one of the best camouflaged.

Busy, hardy and active, with a more upright stance than most ducks, the Khaki Campbell is now a distinct and very popular breed in many parts of the world, renowned for its ability to lay over 300 eggs a year – more than most chickens. It is also a good meat bird, the drakes killing out around five months of age at three to four pounds, and being less burdened with fat than most roasting birds.

From the breeding point of view, one slight drawback is that the ducks tend to be careless mothers, lacking much of a brooding instinct. This attribute seems to have been largely bred out of them in pursuit of record numbers of eggs, and it is generally necessary to hatch off ducklings under an accommodating broody hen.

Chapter Twelve

OUTDOOR FUN AND GAMES

The Severn Bore

From a distance, they look like spindly black ants being sucked towards the plug-hole of an exceptionally dirty bubble-bath, but when you get nearer you can make out a line of athletic wet-suited surfers, zooming upstream on their boards as they ride the mighty Severn Bore, largest of this country's tidal waves, which sweeps some 25 miles up the Estuary between Awre and Gloucester. Some stand upright, arms outstretched, some crouch as they struggle to maintain their balance on the bucking, dipping, careening boards, some – inevitably – fall in and are picked up by the following army of inflatable dinghies. It is a splendid spectacle.

The fashion for riding the Severn Bore was initiated in 1955 by a real daredevil, the much-decorated Colonel 'Mad Jack' Churchill, who had the distinction of being the only British officer to shoot a German sentry dead with a bow and arrow, a feat he achieved during a raid on L'Epinette during the Second World War. Nor was a bow his only unusual accoutrement. He habitually carried into battle his bagpipes as well, and was armed besides with his trusty claybeg – a smaller version of a claymore – like a Highland chief of old.

A line of surfers taking full advantage of the Severn Bore between Awre and Gloucester.

Despite his love of all things Scottish, Churchill was English by birth, and though no relation of the great wartime leader, his surname led to the Germans treating him with particular rigour during his time as a prisoner-of-war. To no avail, though. Twice he was captured and twice escaped, the second time walking most of the length of Italy before reaching the advancing American tanks. His decorations also seemed to come in pairs. He was awarded the DSO and Bar, and the MC and Bar and when, to his chagrin, he found the war in Europe was nearing its end, he contrived to have himself sent to Burma in search of more fighting.

Like others of his temperament, he found peace-time did not suit him. Neighbours complained when he played his pipes late at night, and the chance of finding a live human target for his longbow was reduced to zero. Leaving Britain, he crossed the world to become an instructor in land-air warfare in Australia, and there learnt to surf, becoming obsessed by the thrill of riding the highest foaming waves he could find.

Since this near-legendary figure demonstrated the possibility of riding the Severn Bore, so many others have followed him that there is now a distinct possibility of overcrowding, with too little space for each surfer as the river narrows towards Minsterworth, which is one of the best spots from which to watch this natural phenomenon.

What exactly is a Bore, and why is the Severn's so famous?

The first requirement for a bore or aegir (a reference to the Norse God of the Sea, whose name is a synonym for Terror) is a funnel-shaped river, narrowing sharply, and a very high tide, which causes a large body of sea-water from the estuary to be trapped between the banks. As the incoming tide meets the outflowing river-water, it flows over the top of it, raising the surface of the water up to six feet in the case of the Severn Bore, but in other parts of the world there are bores rising to thirty or forty feet.

In the Bay of Fundy, in Nova Scotia, the highest tides in the world create the Shubenadie River's tidal bore, and China's Qiantang bore, known as the Silver Dragon, can be heard fifteen miles away. The wave reaches 30ft in height, and in 2002 it washed away and drowned 87 people as well as cattle, dogs, and other livestock.

France used to have its Macaret, which swept up the Seine to Rouen, but this was suppressed in 1963 by dredging, and completion of the Tancarville canal. It is still mourned by surfing aficionados.

The world record for surfing a tidal bore is currently held by Sergio Laus, who rode 7.4 miles on the marvellously named Pororoca along the Amazon in Brazil, a considerable advance on 'Mad Jack' Churchill's one and a half miles, but balancing on a surfboard at an average speed of 16mph on the foaming, rolling waves of the Severn Bore for even that modest distance is definitely not for the faint-hearted!

Cheese-Rolling

Human reactions to the sight of a steep grassy bank are entirely predictable. First they want to run down it, taking great leaps, probably falling over a few times, sliding, getting up and running again until they reach the bottom. Or else they long to bowl a large, round, heavy object from the top and watch it bouncing and bounding down the slope at ever-increasing speed. Or better still, to bowl the heavy round object and then chase after it...

The traditional Cheese-rolling and Wake that takes place annually in Spring at Cooper's Hill, just south of Brockworth, satisfies both these desires, and it hardly matters whether it originated as a pagan fertility ritual or a Roman competition, or is simply a recently invented bit of fun. So long as there are tough young men and dashing girls (often from the Antipodes) prepared to risk their necks, ankles, and collarbones in pursuit of a 7 or 8lb round of Double Gloucester cheese and a moment of glory, the rolling is bound to continue, whatever the police or highways authorities may say.

Even when the races themselves were cancelled in 2001, when Foot and Mouth Disease brought the countryside to a standstill, a single cheese was ceremoniously bowled down the 200 yard course, in order to keep the tradition unbroken.

Nor was the event allowed to lapse in 2010, when stern official notices were plastered over the approach-roads, announcing that the cheese-rolling would not take place. As a traffic deterrent this was effective in keeping away the cohorts of spectators' cars which had proved a nuisance in earlier years, but no one can ban people from a common, and the races were run as usual, albeit unofficially.

Over the years the ritual has been honed and polished to a fine degree. There are four downhill races, which include one

Battered but not bowed: a triumphant winner grasps the cheese at Cooper's Hill.

Women competitors set off down the steep slope at the annual Cheese-rolling Races on Cooper's Hill. The cheese – a Double Gloucester – can be seen bouncing downhill at the bottom of the picture.

specifically for ladies, and three uphill, for under-twelve boys, girls, and all-comers respectively. The course itself is extremely steep and rough, with sudden bumps and near-precipices, perfect conditions for breaking bones, and it is rare for no one to need the attention of paramedics.

Around fifteen contestants line up at the top of the hill, where the Master of Ceremonies, stylishly arrayed in white stockman's coat with buttonhole posy and a high-crowned hat adorned with a tricolor ribbon, calls them forward to the brink and then hands the celebrity Guest of Honour the solid round lump of cheese which he or she is to launch downhill.

It is a very special cheese: a half-truckle of Double Gloucester weighing as much as the average newborn baby, and very much harder, especially since it is armoured in a cardboard wrapping to ensure it remains edible after its helter-skelter progress down the hill. It is made by Mrs Diana Smart of Churcham, from the milk of her Brown Swiss, Holstein, and (crucially) Gloucester cows. It is adorned with crossing ribbons, bright red and bright blue, and is a very covetable prize.

'One to be ready!' shouts the MC

'Two to be steady!'

'Three to – prepare!' This is the moment when the cheese is bowled on its way.

'Four to be OFF!' And away go the contestants, hurling themselves recklessly over the edge and down the unforgiving slope. Weight back, legs braced, arms flailing wildly – in the first thirty yards there will probably be four or more fallers, who are well advised to land on their backsides to avoid breaking their necks – and ahead of them all and likely to stay that way is the lean agile figure and curly dark head of that man of iron, Christopher Anderson, virtually invincible in the past few years, and prepared to take many a hard knock without complaint..

It is not unknown for the missile to veer off-course and hit an innocent bystander, but a combination of St John's Ambulance teams and the heroic backstop of rugby players who interpose their muscular forms between the out-of-control contestants and the crash barriers at the bottom keep injuries to the minimum. As the competitors make their way home to nurse their bruises, they vow to be back on the hill next year, and everyone in the crowd agrees that, as a homespun spectator sport, cheese-rolling on Cooper's Hill has few equals.

Chapter Thirteen

ORCHARD AND FOREST

Perry and Cider Making

Brown Bess, Bloody Bastard, Arlingham Squash... The names of Gloucestershire's ancient varieties of pear-tree resound like a roll of honour. These do not produce eaters, but the pears from which perry is made, most of them hard as bullets, thick of skin and unprepossessing in appearance. Some are so tart they dry your mouth as effectively as an under-ripe persimmon, rendering you incapable of speech until you have had a good long drink. They are classified as sweet, bittersweet, sharp, or bittersharp, and each type is needed in the correct proportion to make the rich, satisfying brews of perry – pear-cider – for which Gloucestershire orchards have long been famous. Though never produced in such quantities as cider, perry is a delight to connoisseurs, who go to great lengths to track down the few pubs and restaurants where it can be found.

Like perry pears, cider apples have long pedigrees, with noble names among them reflecting the interest the aristocracy took in their orchards. Varieties in honour of Lords Derby, Grosvenor and Suffield grace the bittersweet cohort, while the Duke of Devonshire is definitely sweet, and so – unsurprisingly – is Sack-and-Sugar. Many of these are now rare, but thanks to the timely intervention of the National Fruit Collection at Brogdale farm in Kent, old species can now be identified, grafted, and saved for

A traditional cider press at the Gloucester Folk Museum.

future generations to experiment with cider-making, just as our forefathers did.

Apples and pears are curious in their inability to breed true. If you plant a pip, it will not produce the same fruit as its parent. Instead, it has to be grafted, by introducing a scion – or cutting – of the desired variety into a wound made on a rootstock belonging to a different variety, or even a different species of fruit-tree – pears onto quinces, for example. By this means it is possible to cultivate a wide spectrum of fruit ranging from ultra-sweet to ultra-sour, all using the same type of rootstock.

Locally made with scant regard to precise quantities, traditional farm cider was strong stuff, and that was how the men

(and women) of Gloucestershire liked it. The labourer who had turned hay with a wooden rake for hour after hour in a July heat-wave, who had ploughed his daily acre in the autumn, or built a yard of dry-stone wall in the cold winds of January would have despised the thin, fizzy, sickly-sweet liquids that are now commercially brewed and passed off as cider. These are all most modern drinkers know, but our thirsty ancestors would probably have tipped them on to the ground in disgust. In centuries past every farm in the

An apple crusher, sometimes known as a 'mill' because of the rotating action of the rolling stone, now on display at the Gloucester Folk Museum. Portable versions are known as 'scratters' locally.

Severn Vale brewed its own cider, with half a gallon a day forming part of an agricultural labourer's wages – and field-workers were renowned for putting away heroic quantities.

In 1910 a Londoner who was looking round a Gloucester-shire farmhouse with a view to renting it was surprised to find the cellar choc-a-bloc with great barrels. What, he asked his guide, was so much cider used for?

'Bless you, sir, ' she chuckled, 'we needs it. My master's son Tom do drink a gallon of cider every night, as sure as God's in Gloucestershire!'

It may well have been the Romans who introduced grafting techniques to improve Britain's small, sour, indigenous crab-apples, and certainly in Anglo-Saxon days some kind of fermented apple juice was drunk in Kent; but the champion cider-makers whose techniques became adopted countrywide were the Normans, and as usual, monasteries were first in the field of production. First to sell it commercially, too.

Soon all the great monastic foundations in Herefordshire, Worcestershire and Gloucestershire had established orchards specifically for cider-apple growing, and even after the Dissolu-tion of the Monasteries it rivalled small ale as the countryman's favourite drink. By the end of the 19th century, there were 18,000 acres of cider-producing orchards in Gloucestershire.

Long before that, there had been efforts to improve English apples. King Henry VIII's fruiterer, Richard Harris, began importing popular and productive varieties from France, and planted a model orchard at Teynham from which to distribute his own carefully grafted cultivars to other growers.

Even so, it took a long time to catch up with the Continent. In his *Discourse of Husbandrie used in Brabant and Flanders* which was published in 1645, Samuel Hartlib criticised the poor quality of the apples used to make cider in England, comparing them unfavourably with those grown in Normandy and Spain. A hundred and fifty years later, in his magisterial treatise on *The Rural Economy of Gloucestershire*, published in 1796, D. Marshall was equally unimpressed by the local brew. '*A palate accustomed to sweet cider would judge the rough cider of the farm houses to be a mixture of vinegar and water, with a portion of dissolved alum to give it a roughness,*' he declared, and was equally quick to find fault with the processes by which it was made.

Knocking apples off their branches with the long sticks known as 'polting lugs' was, he argued, bad practice because '*the criterion of a due degree of ripeness is that of the fruit's falling spontaneously from the tree. Nature is the best judge of this crisis. No art has yet been discovered to mature unripe fruit in any way equal to Nature's process.*'

He was right, of course, and would have been horrified at the modern greengrocer's method of picking unripe fruit and letting it mature in supermarket bins.

Nor, I suppose, would he have seen the old country tradition of wassailing the apple and pear trees during the Twelve Days of Christmas as anything but the excuse for a party. Hot cakes and great flagons of cider would be carried into the orchard, where the revellers would drink the trees' health, and pour libations round the roots as well as down their own throats. Men would fire shotguns into the air and women bang pots and pans, then they would dip pieces of toast in cider and place them in the branches, chanting: '*Wassail the trees that they may bear/ You many a plum and many a pear/ For more or less fruits they will bring/ As you do give them wassailing!*'

There was never anything very exact about the making of farmhouse cider. It was more a matter of production by guess and by God, in the near-certainty that the result would be drinkable – even if it removed the skin from your throat – reasonably healthy, since the typhoid bacillus cannot long survive in apple juice, and alcoholic enough to make you forget life's troubles – at least until the following morning.

After collecting the fallen apples and letting them mature in a heap, the next stage would be to break them up in a scratcher, then tip barrowloads of the resulting 'pomace' – or pulp – on to a layer of cloth or straw in the big stone press. When it was filled with a 'cheese' composed of alternating layers of straw and pulp, it was squeezed down tightly by winding the auger-like screw until all the juice had been extracted and flowed from a runnel at the bottom of the press into barrels.

Sometimes, to give the brew more body, a farmer would drop a few pieces of beef into the barrel, where they would dissolve – and once (it was alleged) a whole family of rats fell down the bung-hole. When that vintage was drawn off, no trace of them remained, but the cider was unusually rich, and much enjoyed. The farmer was delighted, and saw nothing unhygienic in nature's process. 'It had yut (ate) 'em and we'd a drunk 'em,' he told a friend who complained. 'Comes to the same thing, don't 'e?'

The bung was left open to catch natural yeast, and very soon the brew began to ferment, a process that continued for several weeks, with the barrels being constantly topped up to prevent them turning to vinegar. When fermentation finally ceased, the bung would be hammered home – and that was about it. Six or eight months later, the farmer would be drinking his own cider, and so would all his dependants, including the hired help.

So ingrained was the notion of the agricultural labourer of his right to free cider that he would cut up rough if any attempt was made to withhold it. In *By Chance I Did Rove,* his charming memoir of life in the Cotswold village of Sapperton during the early 20th century, the architect Norman Jewson recounts the tale of a very unpopular churchwarden, Mr Gulley, who, having been a minor official in the Indian Civil Service, fancied himself a cut above the rest of village society and was adamantly opposed to strong drink for the working classes. He and his equally toffee-nosed wife employed an old man and his son on their small farm and, 'when harvesting started, these men applied for the customary allowance of beer or cider, then a gallon a day. This was against Mr Gulley's principles (for them) so he would not give it to them. However, it happened that he had discovered on a shelf in an outbuilding a small barrel of home-made blackcurrant wine, left by mistake by a previous tenant. Assuming that this was a harmless teetotal beverage, he gave it to them for their harvest drink.

'As it happened, this was some of *the right stuff,* as the men said afterwards; it had probably been well laced with brandy and had had plenty of time to mature. In fact, if he had given them half a dozen bottles of port from his own cellar, it would have had much the same effect. As everyone knows, harvesting is thirsty work, so the men helped themselves freely from the little barrel, with the result that, towards evening, the old man fell off the wagon and broke his leg.

'There was no telephone in those days, so the son got out his bicycle to ride to Cirencester to fetch a doctor, but in spite of his anxiety about his father's accident, he found himself getting more and more sleepy and less and less able to control his bicycle. He managed to steer a zigzag course for the first two miles, by which time he had forgotten altogether about the reason for his ride and, deciding to have a rest, lay down under a tree by the roadside and promptly went to sleep. When he woke up very early next morning, he was perfectly sober but with no recollection of how he came to be two miles from home, so he mounted his bicycle and pedalled back to his cottage, where he was quite unable to answer his wife's searching questions of where he had been all night!'

Cider apples in a wooden trog, of a type which used to be made widely in the Forest of Dean.

Jewson does not reveal what became of the old man with the broken leg, but it is not difficult to imagine the glee with which Sapperton's villagers must have learned that Gulley, the miserly killjoy, had been hoist with his own petard. Depriving a Gloucestershire farm-hand of his cider was bound to lead to trouble.

Yet even in the early days of the twentieth century, cider was losing its popular appeal, squeezed by beer from below and wine from above, as one aficionado put it. Worse followed during two world wars, when many old orchards were grubbed up and the land given over to cereal crops, while large drinks companies preferred to import concentrated apple juice from abroad and treat it with sulphur dioxide to inhibit the natural wild yeasts before fermenting it with pure yeast cultures. By mixing and blending old and new ciders, a bland uniformity of taste can be achieved, and after sterilisation the final indignity is to add fizziness by artificial carbonation in the bottle.

Full of preservatives, sweeteners, and even added colouring – mass-produced modern cider is a travesty of the time-honoured countryman's favourite drink, but recently the pendulum has reversed its swing: the fightback has begun. If you know where to look you can still find real cider to drink.

Since it was set up in 1971, the Campaign for Real Ale (CAMRA) which has done much to improve the quality of British beer, has produced a splendidly-named offshoot APPLE – the Apple and Pear Produce Liaison Executive – devoted to promoting real cider and perry. Their parameters are strict but very simple: no concentrate, carbon dioxide, preservative or sweeteners. Real cider or perry is essentially the fermented juice of apple or pear, nothing added and nothing taken away, and the *Good Cider Guide* that they publish tells you exactly where each of them is available.

Add to this the cheerful sight of hundreds of newly planted orchards blossoming each spring in cider's traditional three counties of Gloucestershire, Herefordshire and Worcestershire, and the outlook looks bright for the future of the only drink which, according to Captain Sylas Taylor in Evelyn's *Pomona* of 1664, can 'Relax the belly, aid concoction, depress Vapours, resist Melancholy, Spleen, Pleurisy, Strangury, and being sweetened with sugar abate inveterate Colds...'

No wonder farm-workers toasted their trees and wished them long life and good health as they drank their daily (free) half-gallon, for truly cider was a drink with exceptional powers.

The Forest of Dean

An aura of mystery has always surrounded men who plunder the earth's underground treasures, so it is hardly surprising that inhabitants of Gloucestershire's sunny uplands and verdant valleys should regard the miners and charcoal burners, foresters and iron-workers of the Forest of Dean with a degree of awe amounting to fear.

From time immemorial they have burned charcoal and mined the rich seams of coal, iron ore and ochre that lie beneath the triangular plateau between the Rivers Severn and Wye. As F.W.Harvey put it:

In Devil's Chapel they dug the ore
A thousand years ago, and more
Earth's veins of gleaming metal showing
Like crusted blood first set a-glowing
Phoenician faces...

Black-avisaged from charcoal and slack, independent, proud, and immensely strong from digging, hauling and chopping, these miners and foresters lived deep in the ancient woodland that had been reserved for Royal hunting since before the Norman Conquest, practising crafts which had descended through countless generations, speaking a strange jargon unintelligible to outsiders and, since medieval days at least, exercising the special rights which allowed every man to be his own master.

It was in 1296 that King Edward I, living up to his nickname 'The Hammer of the Scots' by besieging the border town of Berwick-on-Tweed, which was then the most important commercial centre in Scotland, sent for miners from the Forest of Dean to sap the town's defences. The bloodcurdling massacre that followed Edward's entry into the town set the seal on his victorious campaign to subdue the Scots, and in acknowledgment of the miners' contribution to his success, he granted free mining rights anywhere within the Forest of Dean (except under graveyards, orchards or gardens) to them and their descendants in perpetuity.

To claim freemining rights, a man has to be 21 years old, born in the Hundred of St Briavels, and have worked for a year and a day underground, and it is only with the closure of the maternity unit at the local hospital, and a blizzard of modern health-and-safety regulations that this age-old inheritance has come under threat. Nowadays if an expectant mother in St Briavels wishes her son to have the right to register as a freeminer, she is well advised to opt for a home birth. Taxes, licences and insurance premiums have also taken a heavy toll and today there are only about 150 freeminers left in the Forest area, but in a curious twist reflecting

Dave Harvey – who was born in the Hundred of St Briavels, and is therefore entitled to make a living from freemining coal in the Forest of Dean – stands with his tools at the 'gale' entrance.

the spirit of the age, a two-year legal wrangle has recently resulted in the registration of the first-ever female freeminer.

Since the age of ten, Elaine Mormon, whose father was a freeminer, has been mining ochre, the iron oxide pigment used in paints and cosmetics since the days of the Romans, bringing it up to the surface in a plastic milk container and selling it for £40 per 250ml. She is now the last ochre-miner in the Forest. As she says, 'I had wanted to be a freeminer ever since I was a little girl, but everyone told me it was only open to men and I accepted that. Then when I reached fifty, I thought, "Why shouldn't I?" The reaction has been very negative. They think I am changing their tradition, but I am not changing anything.'

The Forest's senior official, the deputy gaveller, confirms local male unease with this departure from custom. 'Elaine has been registered but it is fair to say that there is significant disquiet,' he admits. 'The feedback I've had is that a number of people are not particularly happy with this.'

Back in the glory days of the late eighteenth and nineteenth centuries, however, over half the male population worked underground, lying on their stomachs while laboriously hacking out the black gold with picks and shovels, then loading it into specially-designed tubs to be hauled to the surface. The seams, known as 'delfs' were worked from short longwall faces, and the inclined roadways – 'dipples' – had sloping roofs. The mines themselves were known as 'gales' and the miners' activities were regulated by the Court of Mine Law, which sat at the Speech House, where the 'Gaveller' was responsible for leasing 'gales' on behalf of the Crown.

Writing in 1836, the Reverend Francis Witts described a visit to '*the mouth of one of the deepest and largest mines of the district, where the coal is raised from a pit nearly 200 yards below the surface... We watched the ascent and descent of the tram carts, as they were lowered to the bottom of the pit, or raised by steam with a heavy load of coal. From*

Preparing a pile of logs for charcoal burning in the Forest of Dean

Covering the log pile with turf in final preparation of a charcoal burn.

a workman near the pit's mouth, a finely bronzed fellow with intelli-gent and handsome features...and form indicative of great bodily strength, we learned that the persons employed below including boys, amounted to 100, and that eight horses were used at the bottom of the mine who, once admitted, never saw daylight again until age or accident incapacitated them for work...

A diehard Tory, Francis Witts disapproved of the miners' often truculent attitude towards their superiors. Though the busy, swarthy population did not lack for work or money, '*Yet are not these foresters quite easy; they are a secluded, ignorant, but manly and good-humoured race, suspicious as to the purpose and probable results of recent enquiries made by a government commission...which have led to many new plans and regulations which the foresters consider to be infringe-ments on their old forest laws and privileges, which they highly value, and greatly exaggerate...*'

The miners and foresters were right to be suspicious. Twenty five years earlier, in the early nineteenth century, the sudden enclosure of 11,000 acres of the Forest for intensive timber production had led to an explosion of rioting in the local popula-tion. The *Dean Forest (Timber) Act* passed in 1808 to counter the national shortage of shipbuilding material, was an ill-thought-out measure which severely impinged on the foresters' age-old rights. No longer permitted to hunt or fell timber in the enclosed area, nor to mine coal and graze livestock, they formed a committee with the freeminers, determined to wrest back the enclosed forest from Edward Machen, the deputy surveyor in charge of the replanting scheme.

When several days of negotiation between Machen and the foresters' leader Warren James failed to resolve the problem, the angry mob of foresters broke down a long stretch of the enclosing fences, forcing Machen to send for troops to quell the insurrec-tion.

The first round went to the foresters, since the small detachment of soldiers sent from Monmouth swiftly retreated to their barracks when they saw the strength of the opposition, but two days later a heavily armed squadron from the north, and more troops from the West Country, put the rebels to flight.

Warren James was first condemned to death, but later the sentence was commuted to transportation. Although he survived the hulks and was pardoned after enduring five years in brutal conditions in Tasmania, his health and spirit were broken by imprisonment and he died before his fiftieth birthday.

Nor did the enclosure scheme provide the expected benefit to the navy: well before Machel's oaks were mature, naval ship-builders no longer used wood, and most of the controversial timber proved redundant.

The Speech House at Coleford was built originally as a hunting lodge for Charles II. Later it was used for administrative purposes, as the Verderers' Court for the Forest of Dean.

The Castle of St Briavels, on which the industry was centred, was built by Milo Fitzwalter, Earl of Hereford, in 1131 for the Warden of the Forest of Dean, who administered justice from this seat. According to a legend recounted by the bearded Irish poet and wood-engraver Robert Gibbings in *Coming Down the Wye*, the wife of the Governor of St Briavels had to ride naked round the town once a year – a custom that so appealed to lascivious King John that he ordered all young maidens in the town to do the same.

When Milo Hereford was killed hunting in Abbots Wood in 1146, his son founded the Cistercian monastery of Flaxley in his memory. There the monks were granted tithes of venison and sweet chestnuts, and allowed to graze cattle in the Forest. Another of their perks was a forge, together with the right to fell two trees a week to fire it up. After the Dissolution of the Monasteries in Tudor times, the land became privately owned and later still, in 1899, the Crown purchased all rights except for minerals, and Abbots Wood became once more part of the Forest.

With its ancient broad-leaved trees, grassy glades and steep, dark ravines, the Forest of Dean is a place where legends abound, many of them hazy echoes of Arthurian lore, in which Merlin, Morgan-le-Fay, and even the fifth-century warlord Vortigern who invited Hengist and Horsa the Saxons to Britain mix in wild confusion.

In Arthur's Cave near Symond's Yat, for instance, where the remains of hyaenas and sabre-toothed tiger have been found, the infant who would become the Once and Future King was said to have been hidden beneath Vortigern's Hill Fort while Merlin sought for a suitable foster-family for him; while Tennyson's *Idylls of the King* recounts the alarming experience of guileless Sir Pelleas, struck suddenly dumb when he was awakened from a sunny midday snooze beneath a tree's spreading branches by a cavalcade of imperious damsels, heavily armed, demanding directions to the lists at nearby Caerleon Castle.

At Symonds Yat itself, a 500-foot limestone rock round which the Wye winds through a deep, wooded gorge, two ancient hand-pulled ferries still use an overhead rope to cross from the Gloucestershire to the Herefordshire bank and back, and from a viewing platform above the gorge those brilliantly agile fliers, peregrine falcons, with their speckled breasts, barred underparts and tails and yellow legs ending in fierce, black talons can be watched zooming to and from their nests in the cliff face.

As wood lost its industrial significance, the race was on to improve the quality of steel, and here again men from the Forest of Dean were cutting-edge industrial pioneers. Two generations of the Mushet family, working from their foundry at Darkhill, experimented with different additions to the molten iron in the Bessemer converter, or furnace. This used blasts of air to refine the molten iron, a process patented by the inventor Henry Bessemer in 1856, which is substantially the same technique as that used by modern steelmakers.

The strength, light weight and versatility of steel, which could be used for everything from machine tools to railroad tracks, created an insatiable demand. Robert, son of the ironmaster David Mushet, discovered that the addition of tungsten to steel greatly increased its hardness, while manganese increased its ability to withstand rolling and forging at high temperatures.

More interested in experimentation itself than in the practical application of his discoveries, Robert Mushet was left behind while other forge-masters made fortunes by adopting his technique, and it was only through the determined intervention of his sixteen-year-old daughter, Mary, that he was saved from penury.

In 1866 this spirited teenager travelled to London alone and bearded Henry Bessemer in his office to complain that his commercial success was due to pirating her father's research. Well knowing that without using Robert Mushet's method his own process for producing quality steel would not be economically viable, Bessemer acknowledged the truth of her argument and agreed to pay her father the handsome sum of £300 per annum, which he did for the next two decades.

As profits from mining and charcoal production declined, life in the Forest became progressively harder. In the early twentieth century Winifred Foley, whose memoir *A Child in the Forest* was written when she was in her sixties, gives a vivid account of her family's struggle to survive after her father – a miner – was banned from working for seven years as a punishment for playing a leading role in the General Strike of 1926. Cold, ragged, and often hungry, the children became adept at living off the fruits

The Wye gorge at Symonds Yat. The limestone pinnacle in the foreground is called Yat Rock. In nearby Arthur's Cave the remains of hyaenas and sabre-toothed tiger have been found.

The rope ferry at Symonds Yat which still transports people across the Wye between Gloucestershire and Herefordshire.

of the forest, bringing home rabbits, fish, and every edible nut or berry they could find.

Much the same problems beset the three young magicians in *Harry Potter and the Deathly Hallows,* the last book of J.K.Rowling's seven-volume oeuvre. On the run from the Dark Lord, Voldemort – whose name seems an echo of the legendary Vortigern – Harry, Ron, and Hermione suffer hunger, cold, and the corrosive fear of the hunted as they prepare for the final showdown from a temporary refuge in the Forest of Dean, where the author herself grew up.

Although still abounding in deer, as a former Royal hunting preserve should be, the Forest had lost almost all its original boar population before the illegal introduction of cross-bred species of wild boar from Eastern Europe in the past decade. These interlopers are by no means universally welcomed and, in the manner of all alien species, by multiplying rapidly have become a problem for gardeners and householders alike.

With its mines, legends, and myths reaching back into the dawn of history, this ancient woodland region has a timeless, magical quality that is hard to define but immediately apparent to anyone who goes there. It is a very special place – truly a world of its own.

Chapter Fourteen

AND IT'S STILL HAPPENING

The great sheepwalks of Gloucestershire are gone, but the many churches that were built and beautified with the profits of the wool trade still dot the Cotswold landscape, eloquent testimony to the riches supplied by the thousands of animals whose fleeces made England's broadcloth the finest in the world, and Gloucestershire's wool merchants some of England's wealthiest.

Dick Whittington, thrice Lord Mayor of London, once owned most of Stroud, but now the five valleys centred on the town no longer echo to the thunder of mills and reek of sulphur, nor do their streams run red with the dye of scarlet cloth for soldiers' uniforms, green for billiard-table baize, or woad-blue for the merchants' Sunday best. Yet the corkscrew-curled head of a ram, his horns coiled into stylised rosettes, still adorns the cross in Stroud's high street, and Gloucester City's coat of arms, together with beautifully carved sheepskins on the headstones of wool-merchants' tombs, act as a reminder of how the county's family fortunes were founded.

Nothing but random patches of snowdrops – the non-native *Galanthus* – and gooseberry bushes growing in unexpected places on the steep hillsides mark the sites of countless stone cottages where families of spinners and weavers once toiled from dawn to dusk to produce their daily quota of three to four yards of cloth. The bee-line footpaths they trod on their way to and from the mills in the valley bottoms still crisscross the fields, and are carefully preserved as rights-of-way, while the great mills and storehouses have found a modern use as out-of-town shopping malls, or business parks for light industries.

The slave trade, too, has long been abolished, but handsome houses all over Gloucestershire remain to remind the world of the wealth brought to Bristol merchants through those infamous triangular voyages that saw brass wire, pots and pans, and other British manufactured goods transported to Africa and there bartered for captured and enslaved natives, who were then transported to the Caribbean islands and sold in exchange for cargoes of cotton, tobacco, and sugar which were brought back to Britain on the final leg of the journey.

So elegantly simple. So enormously profitable. So deeply, deeply wicked.

It was inevitable that the many prominent merchants and Members of Parliament who owned sugar plantations or shares in slave-trading ships should have reacted with fury to suggestions that the business should be abolished. Not that slave-trading ventures always showed a profit. If the wretched human cargo was packed too tightly for the second leg of the voyage, there was a strong risk that an unacceptable proportion would die of disease, malnutrition, and sheer misery, their bodies tossed into the ship's wake to add to the appalling stench that followed every slaver vessel. Or, if too few could be rounded up in the huge barracoons of West Africa before the ship was obliged to sail, the voyage was hardly likely to return a profit for owners and share-holders.

James Rogers of Bristol, for instance, who had invested in 51 separate slaving ventures, went bankrupt in the 1790s. In contrast Thomas Coster, MP for Bristol from 1734 to 1739, co-owned six slaving ships, and much of the initial cargo of trade goods they carried was manufactured in his own brassworks in Bristol and the Forest of Dean. He became one of the richest merchants in the city. Despite intensive lobbying and protests by slave-ship owners, William Wilberforce and his brother-in-law James Stephens, together with the like-minded group of Abolitionists known as 'The Saints,' eventually prevailed upon Parliament to pass the Act that abolished the slave trade in 1807, while in 1833 slavery itself was also banned by statute.

If one marvels at the beauty of the Grecian portico and Corinthian columns of the grand entrance of Dodington Park in Gloucestershire, or admires the grounds laid out by Capability Brown, it comes as a shock to remember the terrible price in human misery that paid for all this splendour – and the same applies to many of the county's most admired houses.

Like all districts, the Cotswolds has had its economic ups and down, and after the invention of the Spinning Jenny in 1764 heralded the collapse of the local woollen industry, the sky-high wages once earned by weavers were reduced to a pittance by the introduction of machinery. Whole families were thrown out of work, sparking a general exodus from Gloucestershire's country-side.

The price of agricultural produce fell ever lower as corn was imported from abroad, which exacerbated the problem of rural depopulation. Many families emigrated to the New World, particularly Australia, which had changed dramatically in public perception from a land of hellish penal colonies to one of boundless opportunity for anyone prepared to work hard. Unlimited sunshine was also a powerful attraction to those accustomed to long, damp Cotswold winters.

Roaming through near-deserted valleys in the late nineteeth century and regretting the loss of the busy, thriving communi-ties that used to work there, young Arthur Gibbs reflected on the need for government to grant some measure of protection to British agriculture in order to sustain rural life, and even speculated that a 'great European war, or some such far-reaching dispensation of Providence, terrible to think of for those who live to see it, but with all its possibilities for good arising out of evil for future generations', would be necessary if the old villages were to contain so much as a single inhabitant in a hundred years' time. Without some cataclysm of the kind, he speculated that the Cotswolds would revert to being a huge open plain, with nothing but long rows of tumbledown stone walls as evidence of its former enclosed state.

Someone should have reminded him that you should be careful what you wish for. Two devastating world wars later, he might have questioned whether the price paid for re-populating his beloved Cotswold valleys had not been rather too high.

'If only,' he mused, 'the capitalist or wealthy man of business would take up his abode in these places, all might be well. But alas, the peace and quiet of such out-of-the-way spots, with their fascinating contrast to the smoke and din of a manufacturing town, have little attraction for those who are unused to them.'

How astonished he would be today to see how wrong he was! Tumbledown weavers' cottages are snapped up by hedge fund managers for truly eye-watering sums, while millionaire businessmen value the peace and quiet of secluded farms so much that they feel obliged to install electronically-controlled security gates into their yards, and transform former cowsheds, pigsties and paddocks into state-of-the-art swimming-pools, tennis courts, or garages with automatic doors.

Stars of stage and screen cluster round honeypot villages with easy access to the M4, which allows them to whisk from Gloucestershire to the West End of London in less than two hours, or the M5 which brings Birmingham in one direction and Bristol in the other within easy reach for a shopping trip or night out. Indeed, the county's recent explosion in well-heeled inhabitants is in large part due to the construction of these motorways. Where there are customers with money to spend, a network of high-class shops, restaurants, and service providers rapidly establishes itself to cater for their needs, just as it did when the Romans built the big, straight roads – Fosse Way, Ermin Street and Akeman Street – that intersect at Cirencester.

Arthur Gibbs might be less pleased to note the major drawback of this influx of rich newcomers. Too many local

The GCHQ (Government Communications Headquarters) building at Benhall, Cheltenham – known locally as the Doughnut – employs approximately 5500 staff.

people – particularly first-time buyers – are priced out of the housing market of the popular villages where they were born. It is common for a cricket or football team to have no player who actually lives in the village he represents, being unable to afford a house in the neighbourhood where he grew up. It is a pernicious trend which threatens to fragment communities by divorcing young people from their roots; and projects to counter it include forming housing associations dedicated to building modestly-priced houses for local first-time buyers, with an embargo on their selling on these homes to outsiders.

The recent proliferation of business parks and supermarkets on the outskirts of towns such as Bristol, Gloucester, Cirencester and Stroud is another two-edged sword. On the one hand it makes it easier for people to work or shop without congesting medieval streets with modern traffic; but on the other, such developments tend to have a detrimental effect on the old towns, hollowing them out by undercutting traditional shops and businesses, eventually forcing independent retailers to close for lack of custom.

There is no lack, however, of large corporations taking advantage of Gloucestershire's traditional reputation for enterprise and drive. Bristol's slave traffic may have vanished and the docks become more of a tourist attraction than a powerhouse of trade, but Filton is now an important centre for the aviation industry, with thousands employed by British Aerospace, Rolls-Royce, Airbus, and the Government's Department for the Procurement of Defence Equipment.

At GCHQ (Government Communications Headquarters) in Cheltenham, too, the monitoring of cyber communications and terrorist 'chatter' has replaced the languid gossip of Regency bucks and their bonneted belles who once danced in the Pittville Pump Room. Within the protective walls of the building known locally as 'the Doughnut,' sophisticated electronic equipment is deployed day and night to intercept threats to national security,

Beautiful in all seasons: Westonbirt Arboretum has 16,000 specie trees and shrubs planted over 600 acres.

and an army of signals experts, IT super-boffins, and cyber-spies are hard at work compiling a vast database of email and telephone traffic in a project known as ECHELON which, if it ever becomes operational, would be positively Orwellian in its scope.

Such huge projects apart, there is plenty of business activity on a more human scale as new cottage industries spring up to replace those that have had their day. In this respect the internet is proving a powerful tool in the hands of those who want to work from home, particularly in artistic fields. Artists and sculptors abound and there are many local authors, including Laurie Lee, Susan Hill and Jilly Cooper, the Rev. A.W. Awdry OBE, creator of Thomas the Tank Engine, as well as the playwright Dennis Potter.

Some were born locally, some moved or retired to the area, but the same love of the Gloucestershire countryside informs the work of each. The best-selling novelist Joanna Trollope, born in her grandfather's rectory in Minchinhampton, has a particular knack of capturing the nuances of village life and has always felt that the Cotswolds are her real home. 'It gives me not just a sense of rootedness,' she explains, 'but a capacity to value landscape and weather and the rich life of smallish communities.'

Similarly, much of the work of Laurie Lee, whose mother and siblings moved to Slad when he was three years old, is powerfully evocative of Stroud's steep and secretive Five Valleys, the deep peace of their mill streams and hanging woods. His most famous work, *Cider With Rosie,* beautifully evokes the slow rhythms of Cotswold life in the 'Twenties, as experienced by a growing boy.

Very different but equally vibrant are the saucy romps of Bisley-based author Jilly Cooper's imaginary – but all too believable – fast-living, hard-loving Gloucestershire set, who rollick and frolic in and out of beds in the Cotswold stone-wall country where the Roman fashionistas built their extravagant villas and bath-houses – and no doubt behaved much the same.

Spectacular gardens are still the county's particular glory, ranging from the edgy shapes and plantings of the Rococo Garden at Painswick to the beautifully traditional shrubs and herbaceous borders of designer Rosemary Verey's former home at Barnsley, which draws busloads of tourists year in, year out.

Most stunning of all in sheer scale and vision is the 600-acre Westonbirt Arboretum, with its 16,000 specie trees and shrubs, whose plantings were begun by Robert Holford in 1829 and continued until his death in 1892, after which it was further expanded by his son George, who died in 1926.

The Holford family had lived at Westonbirt for several generations, but really made their fortune when Robert's grandfather, Peter, founded the New River Company, which supplied London with fresh water by means of a canal. When, at the age of 31, Robert inherited Westonbirt in 1839, he had already benefited from the Will of a bachelor uncle, who had bequeathed him six estates and a million pounds including, it is said, a wheelbarrow full of gold.

With such wealth behind him, it is no wonder he thought big. His principal passions were for collecting rare books, works of art, and trees, and having commissioned Lewis Vulliamy to rebuild the Regency house at Westonbirt into an enormous Elizabethan-style palace as a suitable showcase for his art collection, he forged ahead with the creation of an equally splendid outdoor showcase for the exotic trees he loved, enlarging the arboretum and adding unusual specimens for the rest of his life.

As MP for East Gloucestershire, he spent a good deal of time in London, where the same architect designed Dorchester House in Park Lane for him on an equally lavish scale. His son Peter, who continued his father's work in the great arboretum, unfortunately died childless, after which the estate passed to a nephew and began to fall into neglect, a process accelerated by the World Wars.

Neither of Robert Holford's houses is now in private hands, but the living memorial of his most famous creation, the arboretum, which has in the years since 1956 been brought back to its former splendour by the Forestry Commission, presents visitors with a magnificent spectacle at all seasons of the year, with the autumn blaze of maple-leaves a particular glory.

And what of the great river, Milton's Sabrina Fair, the magnet for Gloucestershire's earliest traders as well as the source of its commercial success? New plans to harness the Severn's tidal power for electricity generation have faltered recently, much to the rejoicing of those who live along the river banks, and who feared its impact on the millions of wildfowl and fish that breed and feed in the estuary. Others questioned whether the Severn

Eddie the Eagle was considerably heavier than rival ski-jumpers, and his constantly fogged-up spectacles were a handicap, but nothing is more boring to watch than unbroken perfection in sport, and he quickly became the favourite of millions of spectators.

Barrage would have generated as much power as its promoters claimed, or created the optimistically-promised numbers of new jobs, but no one could be in any doubt of the astronomical cost and, since the project has now been put on ice, for the moment those questions remain unanswered.

Old-fashioned methods of fishing the Severn with putcher traps and lave nets are, in any case, on their way out. The conical wicker putchers are now more likely to be used as supports for sweet peas than lined up across the river to trap salmon, and the big triangular lave nets, in which agile and daring fishermen used to scoop fish stranded in the shallows, are very rare – almost museum pieces.

Traditionalists may regret their passing, but few would mourn the demise of the gluttonous elver-eating competitions at Frampton-on-Severn, when gargantuan quantities of the baby eels which had spent three years drifting from their hatching bed in the Sargasso Sea, were gulped down in timed contests as if they were transparent spaghetti. *Autre temps, autre moeurs!* Nowadays when the elvers wash up the river they are regarded as the rare and precious commodity they have become. Captured alive and only by licensed fishermen, they are exported to augment declining natural stocks all over the world, a very different fate from their predecessors in the Severn.

Rich in history, beautiful in landscape, and successful in trade, Gloucestershire has always claimed a prominent part in English life, but it would be wrong to conclude without recording at least one local man who has made his name as an heroic failure.

Michael Edwards, known world-wide as 'Eddie the Eagle,' was at the height of his fame responsible not only for changing a rule in the Olympic Games, but also for being specifically referred to in the closing ceremony, a distinction never before recorded.

Cheltenham, where he was born, is not noted for an abundance of snow but, though heavily bespectacled, young

Michael nevertheless became a dashing downhill skier, and narrowly missed being chosen for the British team in 1984. Determined to compete in the following Winter Olympics, he re-trained as a ski-jumper and, as the sole British applicant for the team, was accepted for the Calgary Games in 1988.

He was considerably heavier than rival ski-jumpers, and his constantly fogged-up spectacles were a handicap, too, but nothing is more boring to watch than unbroken perfection in sport, and for the 90,000 spectators shouting his name at the bottom of the slope and millions more watching on television, Eddie the Eagle's jumps were a thrilling roller-coaster ride from terror — as his gangling figure lurched and wobbled in mid-flight — to exaltation, as time after time he landed safely. Though he finished 58th, he got far more applause than the winner, setting a British record of 73.5 metres. His apparently light-hearted approach to the solemn business of Olympic sport (though he insisted he was always deadly serious when jumping) and the reckless courage that laughed off broken bones and lack of financial backing, made him universally popular.

Despite this truly Olympian spirit, the heavy-handed intervention of the International Olympic Committee, which toughened the entry requirements to make it nearly impossible for him to compete, put an end to his dreams for subsequent Winter Olympics, and now the one-time holder of the British ski-jumping record and the stunt jumping world record (ten cars/ six buses) lives with his wife and children in Stroud, working as a builder and plasterer in his own well-respected firm.

Rich in history and varied in landscape, Gloucestershire holds a special place in the hearts of all who live and work there, and everyone who has ever visited its thriving market towns, stately castles and churches, taken part in its wide variety of country sports, or has simply stopped beside a road to admire the intricate patterns of walled fields and valleys stretching into the distance, takes away an abiding memory of the county's most precious natural asset, the honey-cream oolitic stone which beautifies everything built with it.

In the evocative words of J.B.Priestley, 'it has learned to remember sunlight even when the sky is grey.'

ACKNOWLEDGEMENTS

I am very grateful to all those who have helped me with advice and information in compiling this book, particularly Mr David Smith, former County Archivist for Gloucestershire, and also the Reverend John Cull, Joanne Terry, of the Edward Jenner Museum, David Read of the Soldiers of Gloucestershire Museum, Alun Williams, of Lister Shearing Equipment, Bob Woodward, who created the replica of the Orpheus Pavement, Mrs Laurence Rook, of Beverston Castle, Mrs Rollo Clifford, Jonathan Crump, and Anne Bartlett, of the Forest of Dean Heritage Centre, besides all those who have kindly given permission to reproduce their photographs, or photograph their property.

Most generous of all with his time, enterprise, and photographic skill was my nephew Jamie Lindsay, of Lindsaylocations.com, and his brother Rory, who supplied his professional photographic equipment. To both of them I extend my warmest thanks.

PB

PHOTOGRAPHIC ACKNOWLEDGEMENTS

I am most grateful to Jamie Lindsay (Lindsaylocations.com), my nephew, for his energetic and enthusiastic help in taking most of the photos in this book.

My thanks also go to the following:

The photos of the Woodchester mosaic and the working party (pages 12 and 15) are courtesy of Robert Ludlow.

The Cotswold and Forest of Dean Tourism kindly supplied: photos on pages: 48, 188, 190, 192

Shearing photo, page 63: courtesy of Lister Shearing Equipment.

Gloucester cattle, page 161: courtesy of Jonathan Crump

Khaki Campbell ducks, page 168: courtesy of Chris and Mike Ashton, www.ashtonwaterfowl.net, 01938 554011

Badminton horse trials, page 161: courtesy of Mitsubishi Motors and Kit Houghton

GCHQ, page 202: Crown Copyright, with permission of GCHQ

Cooper's Hill cheese-rolling, page 176: courtesy of Cotswolds and Forest of Dean Tourism

Eddie the Eagle, page 207 and cover: courtesy of Rex Features

Desert Orchid, page 156: courtesy of John Pike/Racing Images.

Cover image: courtesy of Kate Tann.

Concorde, page 145 and cover: courtesy of www.concordesst.com

Richard III, p45 and cover: © National Portrait Gallery, London

Lt. Col. Carne, page 87 and Rev. Davies, page 88: courtesy of Soldiers of Gloucestershire Museum

Woolsack races, page 73 and cover; Tewkesbury Abbey, pages 38, 41; Cheltenham Gold Cup, page 154; Edward Jenner, page 105; Gloucester Cathedral, page 114; Severn bore, page 172: courtesy Larissa Powell, Cotswolds and Forest of Dean Tourism

SELECT BIBLIOGRAPHY

Barratt, John, *Sieges of the English Civil War*, Barnsley, 2009

Calvert, Brian, *Flying Concorde*, Fontana, 1981

Cheetham, Anthony, *Richard III*, Weidenfeld, 1972

Crowden, James, *Cider, the Forgotten Miracle*, Cider Press, 1999

Cull, the Rev. John, *Roman Woodchester*, Pitkin, 2000

Derrick, Freda, *Cotswold Stone*, Chapman and Hall, 1948

Dexter, J.H., *The Reign of King Pym*, Harvard, 1941

Gibbs, J.Arthur, *A Cotswold Village*, Murray, 1898

Grove, Valerie, *Laurie Lee*, Viking, 1999

Harvey, Graham, *The Killing of the Countryside*, Cape, 1997

Heffer, Simon, *Vaughan Williams*, Weidenfeld, 2000

Huxley, Elizabeth, *Peter Scott*, Hamish Hamilton, 1993

Jewson, Norman, *By Chance I Did Rove*, Griffon Public., 1986

Jones, Anthea, *The Cotswolds*, Phillimore & Co, 1997

Kennedy, Michael, *The Works of Vaughan Williams*,
    Clarendon Press, 1992

Lees-Milne, James, *Prophesying Peace*, Chatto and Windus, 1977

Ottaway, Hugh, *Vaughan Williams Symphonies*, BBC Public., 1972

Palmer, Roy, *The Folklore of Gloucestershire*, Westcountry Books,
    1994

Reid, Stuart, *All The King's Armies*, Staplehurst, 1998

Seth-Smith, Michael, *The History of Steeplechasing*, Michael Joseph,
    1966

Verey, David, *Gloucestershire: The Cotswolds*, Penguin Books, 1970

Waters, Brian, *Severn Tide*, Alan Sutton, 1987

Witts, Rev. F.E., *The Diary of a Cotswold Parson*, Alan Sutton,
    1986

USEFUL ORGANISATIONS

Ashton Wildfowl, www.ashtonwaterfowl.net, 01938 554011
– for Khaki Campbell ducks

Berkeley Castle
Gloucestershire GL13 8BQ
Telephone 01453 810332
www.berkeley-castle.com

Concorde Visitor Centre
Main Reception Car Park, Golf Course Lane, Filton, BS34 7QS
www.concordeatfilton.org.uk

Edward Jenner Museum
The Chantry, Church Lane, Berkeley GL13 9BN
Telephone 01453 810631
www.jennermuseum.com

Fairford Air Show
Kempsford, Fairford, Gloucestershire GL7 4RB
www.airtattoo.com

Gloucester Cattle Society
Telephone: 01926 651147 www.gloucestercattle.org.uk

Gloucester Cathedral
12 College Green, Gloucester GL1 2LX
Telephone 01452 528095
www.gloucestercathedral.org.uk

Gloucestershire Regiment

Soldiers of Gloucestershire Museum, Custom House, Gloucester
Docks, Gloucester GL1 2HE
Telephone 01452 522682
www.glosters,.org.uk

Kelmscott Manor

Kelmscott, Lechdale, Gloucestershire GL7 3HJ
Telephone 01367 253 348
www.kelmscottmanor.co.uk

Severn Bore (for timetable)

www.riverseveornbore.co.uk

Slimbridge Wildfowl and Wetlands Trust

Gloucester, Gloucestershire GL2 7BT
Telephone 01453 890333
www.wwt.org.uk

Tetbury Woolsack Races

www.tetburywoolsack.co.uk

Tewkesbury Abbey Office

The Visitor Centre, Church Street, Tewkesbury GL20 5RZ
Telephone 01684 850959
www.tewkesburyabbey.org.uk

TOURIST INFORMATION CENTRES

Bourton-on-the-Water
Victoria Street, Bourton-on-the-Water, GL54 2BU
Tel: +44 (0)1451 820211
bourtonvic@btconnect.com

Cheltenham
77 Promenade, Cheltenham, GL50 1PP
Tel:+44 (0)1242 522878
tic@cheltenham.gov.uk

Chipping Campden
Old Police Station, High Street, Chipping Campden, GL55 6HB
Tel: +44 (0)1386 841206
info@campdenonline.org

Cirencester
Corinium Museum, Park Street, Cirencester, GL7 2BX
Tel: +44 (0)1285 654180
cirencestervic@cotswold.gov.uk

Gloucester
28 Southgate Street, Gloucester, GL1 2DP
Tel: +44 (0)1452 396572
Fax: +44 (0)1452 504273
tourism@gloucester.gov.uk

Moreton-in-Marsh
Moreton Area Centre, High St., Moreton-in-Marsh, GL56 0AZ
Tel: +44 (0)1608 650881
Moreton@cotswold.gov.uk

Nailsworth
4 The Old George, Fountain Street, Nailsworth, GL6 0BL
Tel: +44 (0)1453 839222
nailsworthtic@btconnect.com

Stroud
Subscription Rooms, George Street, Stroud, GL5 1AE
Tel: +44 (0)1453 760960
Fax: +44 (0)1453 755658
tic@stroud.gov.uk

Tewkesbury
Out of the Hat Tewkesbury Heritage and Visitor Centre
100 Church Street,
Tewkesbury, GL20 5AB
Tel: +44 (0)1684 855040
outofthehat@tewkesbury.gov.uk

Winchcombe
The Town Hall, High Street, Winchcombe, GL54 5LJ
Tel: +44 (0)1242 602925 Saturdays and Sundays only in winter.
winchcombetic@tewkesbury.gov.uk

TOURIST INFORMATION POINTS

The following offer a more localised information service (but may
not offer a bed-booking service):

Cotswold Country Park and Beach
Shorncote, Cirencester
Tel: +44 (0)1285 861459

Painswick
The Town Hall, Victoria Street, Painswick, GL6 6QA Tel: +44 (0)7503 516924

Stow on the Wold
Go Stow, 12 Talbot Court, Stow on the Wold, GL54 1BQ Tel: +44 (0)1451 870150
info@go-stow.co.uk

Tetbury
33 Church Street, Tetbury, GL8 8JA
Tel/Fax: +44 (0)1666 503552
tourism@tetbury.org

Wotton-under-Edge
The Heritage Centre, The Chipping, Wotton-under-Edge
Tel: +44 (0)1453 521541

LIST OF PHOTOGRAPHS

INDEX

Also published by Merlin Unwin Books
www.merlinunwin.co.uk

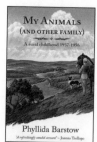

My Animals and Other Family
A rural childhood 1937–1956
Phyllida Barstow

'Her autobiography is psychobabble-free and upbeat. Phyllida and her siblings enjoyed a freedom that contrasts so sharply with the lives of today's over-protected children.' — BBC Countryfile magazine

'A refreshingly candid account' – Joanna Trollope

Hardback 234x156mm   224 pages   16pp   b/w photographs   £16.99

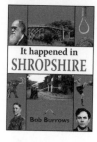

It Happened in Shropshire
Bob Burrows

It Happened in Shropshire is a vibrant and compelling account of the county's diverse heritage; its heroes, its battles, its discoveries, its crimes.

'An invaluable, readable and informative guide to the county.' – Shropshire Life

£16.99

The Otter by James Williams £20
The Hare by Jill Mason £20
Hedgerow Medicine by Julie Bruton Seal & Matthew Seal £16.99
Kitchen Medicine by Julie Bruton Seal & Matthew Seal £16.99
Mushrooming without Fear by Alexander Schwab £14.99
Prue's New Country Cooking by Prue Coats £15.99
Manual of a Traditional Bacon Curer by Maynard Davies £25
Maynard: Adventures of a Bacon Curer by Maynard Davies £9.99
Maynard: Secrets of a Bacon Curer by Maynard Davies £9.99
The Byerley Turk by Jeremy James £7.99
Temptation & Downfall of the Vicar of Stanton Lacy by Peter Klein £12
Over the Farmer's Gate by Roger Evans £12
The Brewer's Tale by Frank Priestley £10
Full English by Edward Miller £7.99
The Countryside Cartoon Joke Book by Roger Penwill £5.99
The Best of BB by BB £18.95
The Countryman's Bedside Book by BB £18.95
The Naturalist's Bedside Book by BB £17.99

Available from all good bookshops